7 WAYS
TO BUILD
YOUR
PENSION

· REVISED AND UPDATED ·
2ND
· SECOND EDITION ·

ANTHONY VICE

howto**books**

Published by How To Books Ltd,
Spring Hill House, Spring Hill Road,
Begbroke, Oxford OX5 1RX. United Kingdom.
Tel: (01865) 375794. Fax: (01865) 379162.
email: info@howtobooks.co.uk
www.howtobooks.co.uk

First edition 2004
Second edition 2006

British Library Cataloguing in Publication Data
A catalogue record for this book is available from the British Library

ISBN 13: 978 1 84528 082 6
ISBN 10: 1 84528 082 2

Produced for How To Books by Deer Park Productions, Tavistock
Cover design by Baseline Arts Ltd, Oxford
Typeset by PDQ Typesetting, Newcastle-under-Lyme, Staffs.
Printed and bound by Cromwell Press Ltd, Trowbridge, Wiltshire

NOTE: The material contained in this book is set out in good faith for general guidance and no liability can be accepted for loss or expense incurred as a result of relying in particular circumstances on statements made in the book. The laws and regulations are complex and liable to change, and readers should check the current position with the relevant authorities before making personal arrangements.

Contents

Introduction

Pensions are what you live off when you have retired from work and no longer get wages or salary. For all too many people, their pension will not be enough – not the traditional two-thirds of income, not even 50%, but for half the UK workforce 40% or less. That spells retirement poverty, and that represents the pension crisis.

This book offers you ways to build up resources in order to afford a reasonable pension. There is no magic formula, but a small number of important practical steps: use the tax-deductible status of pension contributions, and take 25% cash on retirement; build up your tax-free ISAs; take advantage of beneficial schemes such as stakeholder pensions.

The big pension issue of the next few years will be how the government follows Adair Turner's monumental Pensions Commission Report. Turner's strategy is essentially simple: to improve the state pension by linking the pension to earnings, not prices, and by including women on an equal basis from age 75 – breaking the link with National Insurance. To pay for this, pensioners will have to retire later – at 66 by 2030, 67 by 2040 and 68 by 2050, or later still if the government wants to save more. (Public sector employees with their unfunded index-linked pensions, stand happily outside, though there are suggestions that their retirement age will be raised.)

Turner's five key proposals are:

- ◆ state pension age to rise three years by 2050;
- ◆ basic state pension to be universal for men and women over 75, based on residence not National Insurance (women's retirement

age is already due to rise);

- Basic State Pension Saving Scheme to be linked to earnings, not prices, as it was until 1980;
- National Pension Saving Scheme to cover all employees who do not have other pensions – though they will be able to opt out;
- employees will pay 4% of income into this new Saving Scheme, employers will pay 3% and the state will add 1% through tax relief.

One of the great benefits of Turner's plans is that they will drastically reduce means-testing which is inefficient and discourages saving. But there are some tricky issues:

- employers who already pay more than 3% into their pension fund (which many do) may cut back to the minimum;
- small firms with a few employees may find the new pension plans particularly onerous;
- actuaries are saying that Turner has underestimated growing longevity;
- the Treasury claims that the improvements will cost more than Turner believes;
- there is a range of views on who will run the Pension Saving Scheme.

In the meantime you need to take advantage of all the help which the government offers. ISAs are a clear example, plus the tax-deductibility of pensions and the ability to cash in 25% of pension assets. There are other ideas, analysed in the following chapters: take the stakeholder pension – if you set up just the basic plan for 10 years, you will get a subsidy of just under £8,000. Not a fortune, but a help.

You also need to make sure that your financial affairs are sensibly organised. If your spouse has a lower income, then they should hold the shares you buy, so that dividends become tax-efficient; you, not your spouse, should make gift aid payments, and so on. At all times, make the best possible use of your available resources.

Since 6 April 2006 the whole pension system has been made much more flexible:

- annual contributions up to 100% of earnings, with a cap of £215,000 for 2006–7;
- lifetime allowance with a cap of £1.5 million for 2006–7: this is the maximum you can put into your pension arrangements without paying a stiff rate of tax;
- you can cash in 25% of the pension fund which has to appeal more than the alternative of taking taxable income.

It's mostly, but not all, good news: your ability to borrow to buy commercial property in your pension fund has been reduced; there is now an option to draw income from your fund past the age of 75 ('Alternatively Secured Pension') but the experts' view is that the terms are less appealing than a straightforward annuity. The government is effectively offering tax help to take your pension up to around £75,000 a year; if you are more ambitious you will have to operate outside tax-deductibility.

Back in 2003, Gordon Brown proposed to allow residential property – plus more exotic investments – into SIPPS. In December 2005, he made a complete U-turn, so that SIPPS are now suitable for commercial property along with shares and unit trusts.

Always remember: there is no point in investing large amounts of cash in a pension, if it disappears through bad planning or bad performance. You need to be properly organised – that is what this book is about.

The First Step – Understand the Problem

IS THERE A PENSION CRISIS?

Yes, there is a serious pension crisis: very large numbers of people face a much less comfortable retirement than they expect. But no one is shouting crisis. This is because no one has an interest in doing so. When pensioners face up to a bleak retirement in 20 or 30 years' time, today's government ministers will be long gone; no Chancellor of the Exchequer is going to admit that he helped to kill off final salary schemes by a £5 billion a year tax charge now grown to a massive £50 billion.

Anyone in any doubt about the crisis should ponder the following:

◆ The government-appointed Pensions Commission calculates that £57 billion will be needed through higher tax and National Insurance contributions (at today's prices) to ensure that pensioners in 2050 are 'on average as well off as today.' That equals about £1,000 for every man, woman and child in the UK.

◆ 16 million pensioners (half the work force) are facing retirement poverty – surviving on less than 40% of their pre-retirement income (City bank).

◆ More than half of adult workers will be forced to rely on state handouts in retirement unless the government adopts the Turner Commission proposals.

- Already, one out of four pensioners live on less than £7,500 a year – under one-third of the average wage (insurance company survey).

- Four out of ten people over the age of 50 have already been forced to delay their retirement because their pensions are inadequate (Saga).

- 12.7 million people, or 45% of the adult workforce, are making no provision for retirement (government survey).

- Three million people are seriously under-saving, and 10 million are not saving enough (government Minister in Parliament).

- Only one employer in five is now offering a pension scheme based on final salary (House of Lords Committee).

One could go on: if you work in the south-west of England, you have only a one in five chance of a comfortable retirement – defined as having a retirement income equal to 50% or more of final salary. If you regard hardship in retirement as getting less than 40% of final salary, in the north-east three out of five workers will fall into that group. Over the past ten years the total number of workers caught in the hardship group has grown by five million; the number who can expect to retire comfortably has fallen by nearly 3.5 million.

WHAT CAUSED ALL THIS?

No one is admitting to starting the crisis. The culprits include:

1. The near 50% drop in the London stock market 2000–2003, notably including the dot-com collapse.

2. Gordon Brown taking £5 billion a year from pension funds

from 1997 onwards by ending tax relief on dividends – by now, a £50 billion take.

3. Lower annuity rates, reflecting falling interest rates and inflation. Annuity rates now stand around their lowest level for 40 years, and have dropped by more than half since 1990 – with the experts not expecting any short-term upturn. Many people have been hit by a double whammy – their pension fund is worth less because share prices have fallen and the fund earns a smaller pension because annuity rates have come down.

4. People continue to live longer, so annuity rates are pushed down for that reason. And the UK is not even at the top of the first world's life expectancy table – suggesting that further increases in longevity are possible.

5. New accountancy rules have compelled companies to publish the shortfall in their pension funds (FRS 17) which has probably worried employees and led employers to re-think their pension schemes.

6. Workers are changing jobs rather than staying with one employer for their working life: this has a negative impact on pension entitlement.

WHAT HAS THE GOVERNMENT DONE?

Their important positive move has been to make pensions simpler and much more flexible from 6 April 2006. The effect of the lifetime cap (£1.5 million and rising) and your ability to put 100% of earnings into a pension (cap £215,000 and rising) means, for instance, that people in a company pension scheme can top up their plan significantly. The old 15% salary limit and the earnings cap have gone, along with all the age-based restrictions.

In the year you retire, you can make an unlimited contribution to your pension – though you will only get higher rate tax relief up to 100% of your earnings. You can still take 25% of your pension as tax-free cash when you retire. Otherwise, you have to use the money to provide a taxable income – so many people will take the money!

There is even a benefit for smaller pension funds of less than 1% of the lifetime cap – £15,000 in 2006–7. You can now take the whole sum in cash, with 25% tax-free; previously, you had to take an annuity if your fund was over £2,500.

Under Gordon Brown's pension credit rules (which Turner wants to change), you should not save at all unless you are confident you can build up a pension fund of at least £50,000:

When not to save – an example (from Mercer)

Alan Wardle, 65, has just retired on a state pension of £60 a week – below the maximum because he did not make sufficient National Insurance contributions. Alan has also built up his own pension fund, worth just over £40,000, which has been used to buy an annuity so as to give him a further £40 a week. (Alan, a cautious soul, paid in £1,200 a year to his fund, which grew at an annual 5%.)

Alan's pension income amounts to £100 a week, so he gets £5 a week pension credit plus a further £13 as the savings elements of pension credit. But poor Alan has a bad deal: because of the annuity which he bought, he misses out on £27 of pension credit. This means that his pension fund effectively brings in only an extra £13 a week. And to get this £13 a week Alan saved £23 a week, so that his pension savings, allowing for the effects of the pension credit, have in reality given him a loss, of between 5% and 10% a year!

> He would have been better off – looking at his working life and retirement –
> if he had not saved to put money into a pension fund but spent £23 a week
> and relied completely on the pension credit. This is how Gordon Brown's
> rules penalise savings.

The government, unfortunately, has also:

◆ raised women's future retirement age under the state pension
from 60 to 65 to the great benefit of the Treasury

◆ proposed a 'lifeboat' arrangement whereby well-run pension
schemes will bail out those in trouble – which seems certain to
help kill off the remaining final salary schemes

◆ halved the inflation protection which companies must give
pensioners, from 5% to 2.5%

◆ set up a pension credit scheme which is based on means testing,
where one in three miss out.

What about compulsory contributions?

The shift from *defined benefit* (final salary) to *defined contribution*
(money purchase) pensions means greater uncertainty for pensioners
– not least because employers contribute less: 4.3% against 9.9%,
according to the government. Even these rates are higher than the
3% of earnings which Turner has proposed as employers'
contribution. If all employers move to 3%, company pensioners will
lose out.

How we compare

European pensions as a percentage of average earnings:

◆ Holland   100%
◆ Italy   83%

- Greece   80%
- Portugal   80%
- Germany   65%
- Belgium   60%
- France   50%
- Spain   50%
- Denmark   40%
- United Kingdom   16.75%

'SLEEPWALKING INTO A RETIREMENT OF RELATIVE POVERTY'

Overall analysis of pensions is important, but what matters is the impact on an individual. Accountants PwC have done ground-breaking work, with the unhappy conclusion that 'many young people may be sleepwalking into a retirement of relative poverty.'

Take John Doe, age 20 in 2000 and expecting to retire at age 65 in 2045. He is paid average UK earnings – currently around £25,000 a year – and will stay with the same employer all his working life (an optimistic assumption nowadays). If John Doe retired today he would probably get a two-thirds pension, or £16,500 a year. But by 2045 his private pension will be worth only about 30% of his final salary (£7,500 in today's figures) which the basic state pension would improve to only 37%. John Doe would have to depend on means-tested payments from the pension credit to bring his pension up to 40% of UK average earnings: that would still give him only £10,000 a year compared to £16,500 now.

Women suffer even more

John Doe has good reason to feel concerned, but Jane Doe is even worse off. Assume that Jane starts on the same salary as John, but takes a career break in her thirties to look after her pre-school age children. When she goes back to work she faces a triple whammy:

- she lost earnings, and therefore pension contributions, during her career break

- she may also have fallen behind in earnings relative to John Doe ('glass ceiling effect')

- she will face a lower annuity rate on retirement, because women are expected on average to live longer than men.

(Lower annuity rates for women may change if the EU insists that rates are equalised for men and women, but the concern is that rates for men then would suffer as insurers compensate.)

When Jane Doe retires at 65 her private pension, for all these reasons, will be only just above half of John's. The state pension and pension credit will help bridge the gap, but at age 65 her total pension will still be around 20% less than John's.

For ordinary people, this is the pension crisis – which Turner's plans will help, if the government decides to put them in place.

The pension crisis

% of UK average earnings in year when age reached	Private pension Age		Total pension Age	
	65	75	65	75
Average earners				
John Doe (retires at 65)	30	25	39	36
John Doe (retires at 70)	–	40	7	46
Jane Doe (retires at 65 after mid-career break)	19	16	32	30
Low earners – 50% of UK average earnings				
John Doe (retires at 65)	10	8	27	26
Jane Doe (retires at 65 after mid-career break)	6	5	24	24
High earners – 200% of UK average earnings				
John Doe (retires at 65)	80	65	87	71
John Doe (retires at 55)	33	27	40	37

(All earners assumed to reach 65 in 2045; total pension = private + state pension + any pension credit.) Source: PwC

This example, produced by a leading firm of accountants, highlights the bleak features of the present pension scene, and why this has grown into a crisis:

◆ The high cost of retiring early: this is the only difference between the two high earners, yet by age 75 the man who retired age 55 is drawing only around half the pension of the other.

◆ Low earners may be better off staying solely inside the state system. They do not get much from their private pensions (10% or less of UK average earnings) and if they do make private savings, these will be taxed at 40% under the pension credit arrangements.

◆ Women do badly under the present system: using today's figures, the female low earner would be getting only £6,000 a year by age 75 and the average earner £7,500.

◆ Both the state pension and private pensions will fail to keep pace with the growth in average earnings: in none of the seven cases is the pension, expressed as a percentage of average earnings, higher at age 75 than 65 (except for the man who chose to retire at 70 rather than 65).

◆ There is pressure under the present set-up for people to work until age 70 in order to enjoy a decent pension. After five years, the average earner who retired at 70 is almost 30% better off than his opposite number who retired at 65; he is considerably better off even than the man who earned double the UK average when he worked, but who retired at 55.

These figures show that already at age 75, six out of the seven are getting less than 50% of average earnings, and that a majority – four out of the seven – are facing hardship, receiving less than 40% of their pre-retirement income.

$$\bigcirc 2$$

The Second Step –
Work Out a Strategy

Just before starting your programme to beat the pension crisis, you need to make sure that your finances and family tax set-up are sensibly organised. You need to do three things – draw up a budget of living expenses, at least in outline, keep enough ready cash and arrange to be tax-efficient. Many people work to a budget, if only in the back of their mind. The purpose here is two-fold: to provide a target for your pension income to exceed your living expenses by between 25% and 50%, and to indicate how far you should stay liquid.

KEEP ENOUGH READY CASH

Many people make the mistake of over-investing, buying good medium- and long-term assets but leaving themselves short of ready cash. The conventional wisdom is that you should keep between three and six months of your living expenses in liquid assets, which you can get your hands on quickly without penalty or capital loss. This means bank and building society deposits, which gives you an immediate problem: accessibility brings low rates of interest. Standard rate taxpayers will find a number of accounts that keep up with inflation after allowing for tax; higher rate taxpayers will find a few.

There are two ways to solve this dilemma, at least in part: one is to invest in accounts that are available on the Internet – these typically offer rather better rates for savers than telephone or post accounts, which themselves offer more than high street branches. The second part of the solution is to shop around; some accounts will offer bonuses for the first six or twelve months, so you will need to change when these expire. To keep up your income, you have to be prepared to be flexible – otherwise you lose out.

Are you owed a rebate? – an example

Jane Coxon works as a part-time library assistant and was paid £4,900 in 2004–5. She also received £400 interest from her savings. She believes that her earnings have been correctly taxed, but she realises that tax has been deducted at 20% from her savings interest. She asks her husband, who is an accountant, if she is owed a rebate.

His first step is to work out Jane's gross income. If she received £400 of savings interest after 20% tax, then her pre-tax interest amounted to £500: £400/100 -20 – the bank is compelled to deduct tax at 20%, so for her to receive £400 of savings interest her gross income must amount to £500. This means that her total pre-tax income for the year reached £5,400: £4,900 from her job and £500 from savings.

Jane's husband knows that the personal allowance for the year amounted to £4,745 and that 10% tax was charged on the next £2,020. This means that anyone earning less than £6,765 should not pay tax at more than 10%.

As Jane's total income fell below £6,765, she is only liable for tax at 10%, as opposed to 20%, on her savings interest. She should have paid £50 tax on the £500 interest rather than the £100 she was actually charged. The taxman owes her £50.

TAX FOR MARRIED COUPLES

To get full benefit from a crisis-beating programme, you need to have a reasonably efficient tax set-up. A typical example: the husband draws an executive salary while his wife, maybe looking after pre-school age children, has a small or even no income. (The point also applies in reverse, for a high-earning wife and a house-husband.)

The first step is to arrange that income-producing assets, such as bank deposits or shares, are owned by the wife; this can produce significant tax savings with the wife paying no tax or 10% against the husband's 22% or 40%. If the wife pays no tax, there is rather less point in transferring ordinary shares because (since 1997) the 10% tax credit cannot be reclaimed. It is still a good idea to transfer shares if the husband is a higher-rate taxpayer; at least the shares should be put into joint names of husband and wife. This means that the Inland Revenue will share the dividends 50:50 (unless you tell them otherwise) and you have arranged to benefit from two sets of allowances against capital gains tax when the shares come to be sold.

Following this logic, any payments to charity through a covenant or gift aid should be made by the husband, not the wife. There is a danger here: if the wife pays no tax and makes a gift aid payment, the charity will reclaim the tax (which the wife has not paid) and the Inland Revenue will demand the tax back from her!

Coping with age allowance – an example

Alan Lester, 70, had a total income of £26,000 for 2004–5: just over half of this, £16,000, came from savings in high-yield bond funds which Alan has built up over the years. Because his income is over the £18,900 limit for age allowance, his personal allowance is reduced and the married couple's allowance is also cut back.

His wife, Margaret, has only a small state pension, so her income falls well below the £18,900 limit. Alan realises that the solution is what he should have done some years ago – move the funds into joint ownership.

When he does this, he and Margaret each have an investment income of £8,000 a year. His is halved from £16,000 to £8,000, so that his total income falls from £26,000 to £18,000, which is below the age allowance limit. As a result, Alan will now get the full personal allowance for people in the 65 to 74 age bracket and he and Margaret will get the full married couple's allowance.

A useful thought: you can place some assets with your children, and so long as income is less than £100 a year, it will be free of tax. If you can persuade the grandparents – or godparents or friends – to make the gift (be careful to note where the money comes from) the income will be tax-free up to the child's annual allowance.

TAX FOR UNMARRIED COUPLES

In a recent survey, a majority of people believed that 'common law marriages' were legally recognised, allowing heterosexual partners to enjoy the same tax benefits as married couples. Not so: the law has been changed to allow same-sex couples to register and enjoy the same legal and taxation rights as married couples, but this new concept of 'civil partnership' will not apply to unmarried heterosexual couples. (By the same logic, same-sex couples who register will have to make do with one principal residence – previously, they could have one each.)

Transfers of investments between husband and wife, as suggested above, are free from capital gains tax. There is no such exemption for heterosexual couples who live together: for tax purposes they are treated as unconnected individuals, so that the partner making a transfer of shares is potentially liable to tax. The only solution is to make transfers where the gains fall within the annual exemption or can be offset by losses.

There is a major inconsistency in official policy: benefits legislation makes no difference between married and unmarried couples, for example in giving children's tax credit. Tax and related legislation is the exact opposite: in addition to the difference on capital gains tax, there is complete contrast on inheritance tax: lifetime gifts between a husband and wife are tax-free, but there is no such exemption between unmarried heterosexual partners. When a husband or wife dies, all assets go the survivor free of inheritance tax; when one of two heterosexual partners dies, the assets which go to the survivor are fully subject to inheritance tax.

NEW RULES FOR 2006

Now you have reorganised your finances; before you go any further, you need to take on board the new rules which now operate. If your pension assets go beyond the £1.5 million cap (for 2006–7), you will be taxed at an effective 55%.

If your pension assets were worth more than £1.5 million, you will have to register and they will be ring-fenced: you won't be taxed, but you won't be able to add to your fund without incurring the 55% tax charge.

Since 6 April 2006 – A-Day – there are two ways to protect your pension assets. Primary protection will preserve any excess over the £1.5 million limit and you will still be able to make pension contributions – but if your fund grows faster than the limit, ie faster than inflation, you will be taxed at 55%.

Enhanced protection applies below as well as above £1.5 million. Under this scheme, all the growth in your pension pot will be sheltered – but in return you must stop making pension payments.

If you are close to retirement, the choice should be straightforward, but if retirement is still some years away, you should take advice. (If you are in a company pension scheme, you should be able to get advice there; the government is at last relaxing the legal rules which prevented employers from advising.)

YOUR ACTION PLAN

Your action plan is as follows:

- Since April 2006, as soon as your pension assets start to approach £1.5 million, you should stop paying and save for your pension outside your fund, though you will lose tax-deductibility.

- If you are in a final salary scheme, you need to talk to your employer: if your pension assets come close to the £1.5 million, you may have to stop your contributions and your employer may have to reduce or stop their contributions – in which case you will no doubt expect some compensation! Your pension will be valued on a 20:1 basis, so that a pension of £15,000 a year will be taken as £300,000 capital.

The government is in effect limiting tax-deductibility to building a pension fund which at present will generate around £75,000 a year. If your pension fund goes beyond this level, through contributions or skilful investment, you will be taxed at a punitive rate. Savings for your pension will then have to be channelled into shares, unit trusts, property, roll-up funds, second-hand endowments – as described later in this book.

INFLATION PROTECTION HALVED

There is some not-so-good news: people who draw pensions from most post-1997 company schemes will have their inflation protection halved. Under current rules, employers must raise pensions in line with inflation up to 5% a year; the new terms cut this limit to 2.5%, so that whenever inflation rises above 2.5%, pensioners will lose out.

Suppose that inflation reaches 5%; previously, a pensioner receiving £15,000 a year from his company scheme was entitled to a further £750. Under the new rules he could expect only £375.

THE ISA OPTION

These new rules point to a strategic crisis-beater for everyone who is building their own money-purchase pension scheme – put your money into a series of Individual Savings Accounts (ISAs), and switch the proceeds into a pension only when you are about to retire. Pension contributions are tax-deductible; ISAs are tax-free on capital and income. These two routes will get you to the same place in terms of capital – but with the ISA you keep access to your money in the intervening years. You cannot access your pension contributions, nor cash them in nor, usually, borrow against them.

YOUR THREE KEY WEAPONS

Always remember, you have three key weapons to win the fight for a reasonable pension:

- **Compound interest** – 5% doubles in 15 years, 7% in 10 years, 10% in 7 years.

- **Tax-free investments** – mainly ISAs, and there are a number of alternatives: 22% or 40% out of your gain can make a big difference.

- **Tax-deductibility of pension payments**: essential to ensure that whatever you contribute can be offset against your income.

Compound interest

Few people realise the power of compound interest, which is best seen from a table – keep these figures close to your financial plans. It was Einstein who said: 'The most powerful force in the universe is compound interest.'

How £100 will grow

Rate % \ Years	10	15	20	25
2.5	£128	£145	£164	£185
3	£134	£156	£181	£209
4	£148	£180	£219	£267
5	£163	£208	£265	£339

There is a downside to compound interest, which is shown in the effects of inflation. Even if price rises are kept to 2.5% a year, a £100 bill today will have grown to £128 in just ten years. This is why, when looking at bank or building society investments, you need to calculate the yields after allowing for tax and inflation.

But for an investor, going into tax-free or tax-deductible payments, compounding is of great benefit in building up an adequate pension pot.

IS IT WORTH SAVING FOR A PENSION?

Because of the way pension credits work, lower paid workers may decide not to save – especially if their employer already contributes.

Pension Payments – an example

Joe McCool, 29, works for a charity and gets £16,000 a year (around two-thirds of the national average). Generously, his employer pays £2,000 a year into an insurance company scheme. Joe has been so concerned about the pension news that he started to add his own contributions of £1,200 a year – so that the total pension contributions represent as much as 20% of his salary.

Joe has been told that his pension will buy an income of £11,000 a year at age 65 assuming that the plan grows by 5% a year, on the basis that he does not take a tax-free lump sum out of the 25% to which he would be entitled.

Joe is now wondering whether after all he would be better off spending his £1,200 on improving his house, and risk relying on the state in 35 years' time. The decision is hard to call: luckily he still has plenty of time in which to decide.

Investing tax-free

ISAs are the most popular way of investing so that income and capital gains are free from income tax – and do not even have to be notified to the Inland Revenue. ISAs, which are an important tool in building your pension assets, have become moderately complex – a detailed account appears in Chapter 4. Remember: an ISA is not an investment in its own right, but a wrapper or portfolio which brings freedom from tax to whatever it contains.

National Savings, through premium bonds and certificates, are the other major tax-free route (see page 79) as are Friendly Societies, to a smaller extent.

Using trusts

You also need to be aware of the scope for trusts in dealing with a family situation – though Gordon Brown's 2006 Budget changed the rules for trusts.

Just a few weeks later, he performed an extraordinary about-turn. Most important, he dropped his original plan to charge tax when husbands leave assets for their spouses in trust (widely used in a second marriage to leave an income to the widow but, when she dies, to give the remaining wealth to children from a first marriage).

He also dropped plans for a stiff new tax rate when parents left assets in trust for their children to inherit at age 25 rather than 18. There will still be a new charge, of only 4.2%.

Sadly, clarity has suffered in the Chancellor's march and counter-march. There are still concerns that existing trusts could suffer, along with trusts set up for people who face losing the ability to run their own affairs through illness and the numerous trusts set up by grandparents for grandchildren.

The practical advice has to be: if the assets in your trust have reached £250,000 or so – less than the value of an average house in south-east England – or if you think they are likely to get there, then you need to take professional advice.

SUMMARY

◆ Make sure that shares and income-producing assets are held by the spouse who pays the lower rate of tax.

◆ If there are problems in the outright transfer of shares, at least put them into joint ownership.

◆ All Gift Aid payments should be made by the spouse who pays the higher tax rate. If one spouse pays no tax or 10%, they should avoid Gift Aid payments or make certain the charity does not reclaim tax.

◆ If you are an unmarried heterosexual couple, you need to address possible future issues regarding capital gains tax and inheritance tax, where you have no advantages – but also think about keeping two principal residences.

3

The Third Step – Boost Your Pension

UNDERSTANDING YOUR PENSION SCHEME

If you are an employee, a self-evident first step is to add to the pension provided by your employer.

A typical employer contribution is of the order of 5-6% – if they are most generous, your scheme will be non-contributory. Your pension scheme will be **final salary** (also known as defined benefit) or **money purchase** (defined contribution). In a final salary scheme, you receive a proportion of your final salary, maybe as it was in your last year, maybe an average of the last few years – as laid down in the scheme rules. In a money purchase plan, whose size will depend on how much was put in and how skilfully that money was invested, the money is used to buy you an annuity, so your pension will also depend on prevailing annuity rates at the time you retire. In a final salary scheme, you know your future pension, though you won't necessarily know its capital value; the risk falls on your employer to provide you with what has been agreed. In a money purchase scheme, the risk falls on you; your employer knows what it is going to cost them. You know the capital value of your money purchase scheme, and if it is skilfully invested, you could do well; your problem is that your pension is uncertain.

CAN YOU ADD YEARS?

If your employer contributes, then it is probably worth making an Additional Voluntary Contribution (AVC) – unless their contribution is very small or you have reservations about the investment policy. Your AVC can be used in one of two ways: to buy added years or to build up a pot that amounts to a money purchase scheme. All that you pay into an AVC will be tax-deductible. AVCs will also be possible under Turner's proposals.

Added years is a highly attractive option, which is generally offered only in final salary schemes run by central or local government. The way this works is as follows: a typical pension scheme will be based on 1/40ths, so that if you work for 20 years you receive 20/40 or 50% of your final salary. With an added years option, you may be able to extend your 20 years service to a deemed 25, which will increase your pension by 25%.

There are two great advantages to the added years option. As you are extending a final salary scheme, the risk remains with your employer, not with you. The second advantage is that you benefit to an extra degree from any salary increase you receive shortly before you retire.

CHOOSING YOUR AVC

If an added years option is not available, your AVC will become a money purchase scheme that will grow alongside your final salary pension. Most AVCs are in-house, which means that you save through one of the options offered by your employer. You will be offered the chance to put your money into the employer's fund with the option of an insurance policy or a building society deposit. If you choose the building society, the interest will accumulate grossed-up, which will be a useful benefit over the years – but without the growth possibilities of equities or property.

Your AVC does not have to be allied to your employer's scheme; you can go to an insurance company and buy your own, which is the Free-Standing (FS) AVC. Going to the marketplace probably means that you will pay higher charges, but an FSAVC may appeal to you if you are not happy about the performance of your employer's fund. (FSAVCs were at the centre of the pensions mis-selling scandals of the 1980s and 1990s, when people were persuaded to leave sound employer pension schemes; but that is now history.)

HOW MUCH CAN YOU INVEST?

Now, members of a defined benefit scheme enjoy the same freedom as everyone else. This means that you can invest 100% of earnings, up to £215,000 for 2006–7. You can place the money, over and above what you put into your employer's scheme, into any pension you choose.

LIMITS ON AVCS (UP TO 2005–6)

You might think that you could set aside 15% a year in an AVC, invest it wisely and reap the benefit. Alas, the Inland Revenue places limits on your AVC, so that it becomes possible to save too much – and there is a tax penalty if you do so.

The first hurdle set by the taxman is that you cannot draw more than two-thirds of your taxable income after 20 years' service. So if your AVC fund has grown, and especially if you decide to retire early, you could find that your AVC fund is too large.

The second hurdle is that anyone who joined a pension scheme over the past 17 years is limited by the 'earnings cap'. This cap, which was set at £105,600 for 2005–6, increased each year in line with prices. Any AVCs you set up must not take your contributions to more than 15% of the cap. (Again, all these rules will be overtaken by the new £1.5 million lifetime cap. From 2006–7, though some people will have tax issues outstanding from previous years.)

No cash lump sum

The main drawback to AVCs is that until now you could not take a tax-free lump sum, which is normally up to 25% of your pension fund, unless you started your plan before 1987 (there is an exception for added-years AVCs).

A major improvement in AVCs and FSAVCs will mean that anyone in an occupational scheme, whatever their salary, will be able to contribute to a stakeholder plan.

This will bring the ability to cash in 25% of your pension assets when you retire. Most people are likely to switch to a stakeholder, and AVCs and FSAVCs seem likely to die away.

Pension contributions – an example

Aubrey Smith, age 57, is planning to retire. Under the old rules – changed from April 2006 – he is allowed to make a pension contribution of up to 35% of his net relevant earnings.

Aubrey, who is the finance director of a listed property company, is paid £130,000 a year. He is advised that he must ignore that part of his salary which is above the earnings cap, which has been set at £105,600 for 2005–6.

The maximum pension contribution he can make, and get tax relief, is therefore 35% of £105,600, which amounts to £39,960.

SOLVING THE PROBLEM

The single key proposal to ensure a reasonable pension is that you build up your ISA portfolio and then switch this portfolio into a pension contribution, probably spread over five years, before you retire. Under the new rules, you can invest as much as you want in the year you retire, but higher rate tax relief is limited to earnings.

There are three elements in this operation: first, your ISAs are free from tax; second, your pension contributions are tax-deductible; and third, you can cash in 25% of your pension.

HOW TO EARN 15% PLUS

This basis of this operation is set out in the example below. You decide to make a pension contribution of £20,000. If you are a higher-rate taxpayer, you get relief at 40%, so that the net cost to you is £12,000 after £8,000 of tax relief. You then take the maximum cash allowed, which is 25%, or £5,000 in this case; both the amount of your pension fund and the net cost are reduced by £5,000. The rates of return are so attractive it might pay to consider borrowing.

At this point your fund stands at £15,000, but has cost you only £7,000. You buy an annuity – for example, a level annuity for a man age 65 on a single life. At the time of writing, you could get an annuity rate of just over 7% to give you £1,063 a year. On your £7,000 outlay, that represents a return of 15%, around five times the rate of inflation. You have beaten the pension crisis!

HOW TO EARN 10%

This staggering rate of return is reduced if you pay standard-rate tax, because you get relief at 22% rather than 40%. If you are a standard-rate taxpayer and make the same contribution, your £15,000 fund would have cost you £10,600, so that the £1,063 a year would still give you a yield of 10%. And these annuity payments are coming from major insurance companies, so the risk is low.

The yields are also reduced if you choose a retirement age of 60 rather than 65 – but they still remain highly attractive. On your £15,000 fund the annuity at the earlier age would be £947; that would give the higher-rate taxpayer a yield of 13.5% and the standard-rate payer 8.9%. By any standards, these are crisis-beating returns! (One word of caution: the 2006 budget introduced rules to limit people's ability to recycle tax-free cash into future tax-deductible pension contributions.)

Solving the problem – an example	
1. You make a pension contribution of, say	£20,000
2. You get tax relief at 40%	£8,000
Net Cost	£12,000
3. You cash in 25% of the pension	£5,000
Net cost of your £15,000 pension fund	£7,000

Assume you are a man, aged 65,
looking for a level annuity on a single life.
At the time of writing, your £15,000 would
bring you   £1,063 a year

On your £7,000 net outlay, this represents
an annual return of   15.2%

[Note: this example assumes a higher-rate taxpayer. For a standard-rate taxpayer making the same purchase, the net cost of a £15,000 fund would be £10,600 because his tax relief is worth less. His annual return would still be in double figures, at 10%.]

SUMMARY

◆ Under the new pension rules, build up your ISAs over the years, switch them into pension assets shortly before you retire, and draw 25% in cash. Think about borrowing to boost your pension.

◆ If you are attracted by an AVC plan, check it offers added years.

◆ If you have a post-1987 AVC, switch to a stakeholder so that you can cash in 25%.

◆ Monitor the performance of the funds where your AVC is being invested.

◆ If you are considering a Free-Standing AVC, check out costs and charges before you commit.

STAKEHOLDERS – PENSIONS AT A DISCOUNT

Mention stakeholder pensions and everyone will tell you that they have been a flop – the great majority of company stakeholders are empty and investments made by individuals have included transfers as well as new money. But your friends may not tell you – or may not even appreciate – that stakeholders are a valuable way to help improve your pension assets.

Stakeholders were created by the government in 2001, featuring a 1% cap on charges (now raised to 1.5%), a low minimum contribution and flexibility to stop, re-start or move your plan. But the key new feature, which makes them so helpful as a crisis-beater, is that for the first time you do not need an income to save for a personal pension. You can take out a stakeholder if you are unemployed or if you have no income at all; someone else, say your husband or wife, can set up a stakeholder pension for you. This is where stakeholders start to get interesting.

Over 10 years the taxman gives you almost £8,000!

Everyone who is eligible can pay up to £3,600 a year into a stakeholder pension and get a tax benefit at standard rate of 22% which equals £792. The way this works is that you pay the bank or insurance company £2,808 a year and the Inland Revenue sends them the other £792.

So you have made a pension contribution at a 22% discount: every £100 of pension assets you acquire costs you £78. If you contribute for say 10 years, the taxman will have made you a gift of £7,920! So how do you get your hands on this useful – and rare – gift?

How to get tax back even if you don't pay it – an example

Mary Halliday is a widow who lives with her son and daughter-in-law. She has only a small income, so does not pay any income tax.

Her savings are all in National Savings Certificates – because absolute security is her great concern – but she decides it would be a good idea to make a small payment into a stakeholder pension scheme.

So she gives the insurance company £100. This is regarded as a contribution from which tax has already been deducted, at the standard rate of 22%. The insurance company then goes to the Inland Revenue and claims the difference: this amounts to £28.20, because Mary's contribution is valued at £100 (net, i.e. £100/100–22).

So Mary finds that she has made a stakeholder pension contribution which amounts to £128.20, which has cost her just £100. And the extra comes in the form of a tax repayment, which she received even though she does not pay any tax!

WHO CAN QUALIFY?

The first step is to establish who is eligible for a stakeholder. The short answer is any UK tax resident, but there are two important exclusions:

1. Those who are paid more than £30,000 a year and are members of a company pension scheme, though this restriction is being modified.

2. Controlling directors, whatever they are paid – defined as someone who with family and associates controls more than 20% of a company's capital.

As this is a pension scheme, which must be invested by age 75, you enjoy the usual pension scheme facility of being able to take up to 25% tax-free in cash; the rest must be used to buy an annuity or an ASP.

A family arrangement

Take the case where the husband earns £40,000 or more, while the wife has a modest income and pays little or no tax. In this situation, the husband could finance a stakeholder plan for his wife, which would have two beneficial effects. First, the family would capture the £792 a year which the taxman is prepared to give away.

Suppose that the plan started when she was 45 and she took the annuity at 55 (under present rules, the pension cannot be taken before age 50, which will rise to 55 in 2010) then the gain, at the Inland Revenue's expense, will have been £7,920.

The second reason why this is so attractive is that the wife will pay little or no tax when she comes to draw the annuity – having remembered, one hopes, to have taken 25% of the fund in cash rather than taxable income.

The family faces the double benefit of getting a subsidy from the taxman, a useful cash sum, plus an annuity income which will be wholly or substantially tax-free. This benefit could be threatened by a drop in annuity rates, but many people now believe that a rise is more likely.

This 22% subsidy is a useful weapon in the fight to beat the pension crisis.

Gifts: how to square the circle – an example

Richard Whitcomb, 75, is a widower who lives on a state and moderate-sized company pensions. The mortgage on his house has been paid off and he has built up £180,000 which has been put into banks and building societies, so that the interest supplements his pension income.

Richard's only relatives are his two nephews, who have both just married and would like to buy houses. What can Richard do to help?

He has made his nephews beneficiaries in his will, but that will not give them any money until he dies. He could hand over the £180,000 savings he has accumulated, but Richard thinks he will need at least some of this to live on.

So Richard works out a compromise. He gives the nephews half of his total savings, £45,000 each, and he puts the other half into a purchased life annuity. This is taxed on a more generous basis than a compulsory purchase annuity, so he faces only a small reduction in income. At his age the terms are relatively attractive.

Richard appreciates that he has given up control of his funds and that the annuity income will decline in real terms as he grows older. He finds these drawbacks acceptable: what he wants to do is live for another seven years so that the gifts to his nephews become free of inheritance tax.

What about children?

It is possible to have stakeholders set up for your children as well as for your spouse. The financial advantages remain, but there are some complications. The first is that your children's stakeholder should ideally be financed by grandparents or by uncles and aunts. The second complication is the cash-in age of 55 (unless your offspring becomes a professional athlete, when the Inland Revenue will allow a lower age).

But the tax subsidy is there, so that a stakeholder for children could form the basis for a future pension fund, which they can build on as they follow their own careers. If you and your family follow this route, the stakeholder should be invested in long-term assets which one hopes will prosper over this sort of time-horizon – say index tracker funds.

BUYING A STAKEHOLDER PENSION

Stakeholder pensions are sold by the same banks and insurance companies that market pensions as a whole, but you may find the range of providers rather limited and you will not find much advertising nor a great deal by way of advice. The reason is simple: the government's cap on charges leaves little scope for the providers – by contrast, for example, with companies which sell unit trusts or with-profit bonds.

You need to monitor performance, as you would with any investment. You will receive a statement once or maybe twice a year, but you can generally access your fund at any time by telephone or via the Internet.

Using an intermediary

So how do you buy stakeholder pensions? Many people will go direct to the bank or insurance company, which will be one of the household names – wrong! You can do better. You should go to an intermediary, perhaps the firm that cut the commission on your unit trusts. In stakeholders, they will offer one of two inducements:

1. A straight, if rather modest, cash payment.

Stakeholder pensions – an example

Michael and Susan Spreckley set up a stakeholder plan for Susan, aged 45. They propose to continue for 10 years, when she will cash in, take the 25% in money and draw a pension. They pay £2,808 a year for a policy worth £3,600.

They put the premiums into the insurance company's tracker fund, which they expect to grow by 5% a year. At the end of 10 years, the pension fund will be worth £45,000 and will have cost the family £28,080.

Susan takes 25% in cash, which equals £11,250, so the cost to the family works out at £16,830. She will then have a pension fund of £33,750. They aren't betting on any improvement in annuity rates, so they expect Susan will get a pension of nearly £1,950 a year.

Michael and Susan reckon that as Susan's pension of £1,950 (she has small investment income, so pays tax at only 10%) cost £16,830, the two of them managed to earn 11% gross on the family money. They regard this income as completely safe, as it comes from one of the leading UK insurance companies, and Susan gets to keep 90%. Michael and Susan are happy.

---

2. Of greater interest for the long term, a deal so that the insurance company charges you say 0.75% or 0.85% rather than the maximum permitted.

All this may seem small change, but we are now in a low-inflation low-growth environment where equities are expected only to produce single-digit performance. Never forget: the investment world has changed since the 1990s, and what were formerly modest returns are becoming more significant.

THE ROLE OF THE STAKEHOLDER PENSION

The principal snag about a stakeholder is that it is a pension. You lose control of your money once you invest, and you can only draw it in the form of an annuity once you reach age 55 – you must do so by the time you reach age 75.

Stakeholders are not a substitute for growing your portfolio of ISAs; they have appeal in setting up a pension plan on attractive terms for your low tax-paying spouse or for your relatives to do the same for your children. Many providers offer tracker funds for stakeholders, so you should think of your pension as buying trackers at a discount.

Welcome flexibility

Stakeholders offer the usual advantage that you can cash in up to 25% when you decide to realise. And the welcome flexibility of a stakeholder (you can stop, re-start or change your insurance company when you wish) means that you can take action if you happen to have chosen a bank or insurance company whose funds do not perform well. Here, you are better placed than with a traditional pension or an endowment policy.

Thanks to their tax benefit and flexibility, stakeholders have a useful, if modest, role to play in beating the pension crisis – even if their role is rather different from what the government originally intended a few years ago.

MANAGING YOUR RETIREMENT FUND

Your basic strategy, to recap, is to build up ISAs which you switch into a pension when you retire – £7,000 a year for yourself or £14,000 a year if you include your spouse or partner. But in addition you may want to build up your own retirement fund: what are the mechanics?

Running it yourself

If your employer operates an attractive scheme, which is non-contributory, you could put 15% of your salary into an AVC up to 2005–6. Many people go to an insurance company (nowadays they could also go to an investment trust) for a traditional-type retirement plan.

But you may feel with the new freedom of 2006, that you want to take charge yourself of your pension assets. In that case you could think of a **SIPP** – a self-invested pension plan. And whichever route you choose, the tax breaks are the same: until now, you could invest a proportion of your salary depending on your age: under 35s could pay in up to 17.5%, with maximum 40% for people between 61 and 74. The Inland Revenue set a cap on the amount of salary which is eligible – £105,600 for 2005–6.

Meeting the costs

Until recently, a SIPP was confined to larger funds: you had to face set-up costs and annual management charges, plus dealing costs and advisory charges if you felt you needed outside help. Execution-only brokers have brought down the cost of SIPPs. You will probably operate on-line or by telephone. Overall, your fund should probably have reached £100,000 to set up a SIPP.

SIPPs also have the advantage of flexibility. Some people who own their own companies use a SIPP to buy their business premises. (A SIPP which invests in property should be larger than the minimum size.) You can buy a new property and let the property to your own business. In this way you can turn your office into a pension. The rent has to be set at a market level, but the money goes into your pension fund where it will grow free of tax. When the SIPP sells, the capital gain will be free of tax.

If you invest in property, the benefit of tax relief means that you are buying at a 40% discount. A calculation shows that on a £120,000 property bought through a pension fund, rented out over 10 years and sold, the proceeds could be double those if bought direct.

Some DIY rules

Low-cost SIPPs will appeal mainly to people who want to manage their own fund – and are therefore prepared to invest the necessary time and energy. Because paying an adviser can be expensive, a number of organisations have devised packages: a stockbroker might offer a low-cost SIPP if you agree to take their investment advice; some insurance companies will offer a low-cost deal where you can buy listed shares; and investment trusts offer pension savings plans.

Other reasons for choosing a SIPP

There are two other reasons why experts may suggest that you set up a SIPP. If you are in a final salary scheme, the life insurance cover is limited by Inland Revenue rules to four times salary. If you feel that would not be enough, then you could set up a personal pension where life insurance is linked to the size of the fund; if your fund grows large enough, the death benefits could be higher.

The second reason for thinking of a SIPP is the exact opposite – where you are not married, have no partner and no dependent children. A typical final salary scheme will provide a two-thirds pension (the maximum the Inland Revenue allows) for a surviving spouse and/or dependants. In this situation, a single person without dependants is in effect subsidising the married members, so that a switch to a SIPP could bring a financial benefit.

SUMMARY

♦ Stakeholder pensions give you a subsidy: you pay net after deducting standard rate of tax, now 22%, so that the basic stakeholder policy of £3,600 a year costs you £2,808.

♦ Consider a stakeholder policy for your spouse who pays no tax or low tax, and so will benefit from pension income.

♦ Think about stakeholder policies for your children, set up by their grandparents, godparents or friends.

♦ Buy your stakeholder through an intermediary – get better terms than going direct.

♦ As your fund grows, think about a SIPP, a self-invested pension plan – especially attractive if you invest in commercial property.

4

The Fourth Step –
Grow Your ISAs

The tax-free Individual Savings Account is your most important single weapon to put together adequate pension assets. Your aim is to build up ISAs year after year; shortly before you retire you will switch these into a tax-deductible pension plan up to the amount of your annual salary, with an initial cap of £215,000, subject to a maximum of £1.5 million and no maximum in the year you retire.

An ISA is a tax-free vehicle, or wrapper, into which you can place a wide range of investments. You can invest up to £7,000 a year in an ISA and your spouse can do the same; a family unit therefore has scope to invest up to £14,000 each financial year (April to April) free of tax.

KEY FEATURES OF ISAs

Key features of an ISA include:

- Your permitted £7,000 a year is not carried forward – use it or lose it.

- Joint holdings are not allowed under the government rules; each spouse can have a separate holding.

- There is no limit on the amount you can invest in ISAs during your lifetime.

◆ There is no official minimum amount you can invest – though you may find that one is set by suppliers in the marketplace.

MAXI AND MINI ISAs

You have a choice in how to make your annual ISA investment. You can place your current £7,000 with a single manager, which gives you a **maxi ISA**. Alternatively, you can put your £7,000 with different managers, giving you **mini ISAs**. If you choose mini ISAs, you are restricted to £3,000 in cash, and £4,000 in shares and unit trusts – from different providers if you wish. In a maxi you can put all your £7,000 into shares or unit trusts, which is what many people tend to do.

You have to be 18 to take out an ISA, or 16 for a cash mini ISA.

TESSA-ONLY ISAs

TESSA-only ISAs are entirely separate from maxi and mini ISAs, and the amount you hold in one group does not affect the other. TESSA-only ISAs apply to tax-exempt special savings accounts, which were taken out before April 1999 and have reached the end of their five-year term.

You can invest the capital which you put into the TESSA, up to the maximum of £9,000, into this special ISA. The interest from the TESSA is paid over to you; it is free of tax on coming out of the TESSA.

THE TWO ELEMENTS OF ISAs

There are two elements you can place in an ISA, namely shares and unit trusts, plus cash.

Share ISAs

You can invest in company shares, unit trusts and investment trusts, not just in the UK, so long as the shares are listed. Just how you should spread your investments will be discussed in the next chapter.

Because of the tax change from April 2004, investors who pay tax at standard rate should generally hold their shares and share unit trusts outside an ISA. The fund manager used to be able to reclaim the 10% tax on dividends, but this has been scrapped. There is no longer any tax advantage on dividends – capital gains are still tax-free if your gains go beyond the annual limit – and you could simply be paying the management charge on your holdings. (Higher rate taxpayers still benefit.) But the 20% tax deducted from bond interest can still be reclaimed, which makes bond funds especially suitable for an ISA.

Cash ISAs

Cash ISAs became popular when ordinary shares were falling. They are available from many banks and financial institutions, offering a tax-free rate of interest with security of your capital. The rates offered to investors are often better than typical high street savings rates, while the minimum investments are set low and you can generally get speedy access to your money.

But remember: if you set up a £3,000 cash mini ISA and then have to withdraw the money, you cannot set up another cash mini ISA until the following financial year. You have to watch to make sure that you are getting an attractive rate of interest. You can switch your cash ISA to another bank or building society, but check whether transfer penalties are imposed.

Investing in ISAs – an example

Eleanor Stewart, aged 45, already holds some shares so decides to put a higher-yielding bond into her ISA. She buys a maxi ISA, investing £7,000, with the fund yielding 7%. The manager can reclaim all of the tax deducted from interest payments.

Eleanor goes to a discount broker who gives her a cashback of £50, which covers part of the first year's management costs. He is an execution-only broker who does not offer advice. She has avoided any initial charge; there is a penalty if she cashes in during the first five years – but Eleanor plans to hold the ISA until she retires at 55.

As Eleanor pays tax at the higher rate, she calculates that she would have to earn 12% gross to beat 7% net. The fund pays interest monthly, which would be good for her cash flow if she withdrew the money, but she decides to save by ploughing the interest back into the fund. She also calculates that 7% a year will double in 10 years, which is when she wants to retire and will switch the ISA into a pension plan. And on top of the doubled value through compound interest, she hopes there may also be some capital appreciation.

THE CAT STANDARD (CHARGES, ACCESS, TERMS)

When ISAs were introduced, replacing PEPs and TESSAs, the government set up a kite-mark standard on CAT – charges, access and terms. The CAT standard, which was voluntary, proved of little practical value and has now been dropped, but it still makes sense to check the manager's charges.

HOW TO BUY YOUR ISA

When you put money into a cash ISA, the transaction is straightforward: you contact the bank or building society and fill in the rather elaborate form. But if you are buying unit trusts to put into a mini and especially a maxi ISA, there are some attractive cut-price possibilities, through either a discount broker or a fund supermarket.

A typical unit trust will charge you a 5% initial fee plus an annual 1–1.5% management fee. So if you go direct to the unit trust group, in the first year you will pay about £450 by way of commissions and charges out of your total £7,000 investment. If you are looking for investment performance of 5–6% a year, then you will have lost all of your first year's growth.

Part of these commissions go to brokers, and some of them will share these with you in order to attract your business. They will offer you a bonus in the form of extra units; if that takes you over the present £7,000 legal limit, then they will simply hand back cash. In the present world, where ordinary shares are expected to yield only single-digit growth, costs have become much more important. (Some brokers will even share the annual 'trail' commission they get from the manager.) You can readily access discount brokers through the Internet.

You can drip-feed

Fund supermarkets are an alternative to the discount broker: the supermarkets offer a wide variety of funds (possibly several hundred) along with sizeable reductions in the initial charge. You can even 'mix and match' through a supermarket, by choosing funds from several unit trust groups and putting them into the same ISA. Brokers often offer low-cost packages they have put together.

You don't have to invest your £4,000 or £7,000 in shares and unit trusts all at once. You can drip-feed, what the City calls pound-averaging: you spread your investment over the year in, say, twelve equal contributions. When stock markets are volatile, pound-averaging can represent a sensible investment policy, getting you as near as possible to buying at the market's low point!

You can self-select

Within the official limits you can set up your own self-select ISA: some investors have taken the £7,000 permitted in a maxi ISA and put the money into individual shares or a mix of funds.

There is an obvious appeal in setting up your own investment mix, as opposed to buying a package. The drawback is also obvious: cost. Virtually any one-off will cost you more than a standard product. You should reckon on around £50 a year to run a self-select ISA, a facility which a number of brokers now offer and competition is bringing better terms.

You need to do the calculation to see where this will leave you in terms of net income (this calculation is especially important for standard rate taxpayers now that the government has ended the credit on dividends). Your capital gains will still be free of tax, assuming that you expect to make more than the annual tax-free limit.

SOME ISA DON'TS

The ISA rules are moderately complex, though you can get help from an intermediary or the company or unit trust group where you are investing. But there are some potential pitfalls:

◆ Don't open two maxi ISAs in the same tax year – if you find that you have, tell your ISA manager.

◆ Don't open a maxi and mini ISA in the same tax year.

◆ Don't try to transfer shares you already own into an ISA: the official rules oblige you to sell the shares, put the money into the ISA and then buy the shares back from within the ISA – all of which means you pay dealing costs and possibly capital gains tax.

◆ Don't try to open a joint ISA: these are not permitted – you and your spouse can have an ISA each.

◆ Don't make ISA contributions if you move abroad – but you will still benefit from the ISAs you set up before you left the UK.

If your employer has a company share scheme

Shares that mature from some approved company share schemes can be moved to an ISA free from capital gains tax, as part of the £7,000 a year. This is a useful option for the longer term, unless you have doubts about the future of the company's share price!

The shares have to be transferred within 90 days from the date of exercise, and they will be valued at their current market price: if they are quoted at £5, then you can transfer up to 1,400 into your ISA.

GETTING YOUR MONEY OUT

The official rules do not present any obstacles to your withdrawing your money – but ISA managers may work differently. In both maxi and mini ISAs, the manager may impose a time delay, or make a charge: this is something you need to check before committing yourself.

The official rules, for once, are simple: the controls operate only on the amount you can put in, not what you take out. The rule is that your contributions must not exceed your annual allowance. So if you put £7,000 into a maxi ISA, and later withdraw £2,000, you cannot invest any more until the next financial year. If you put £5,000 into a maxi ISA and withdraw half of that, you are limited to £2,000 of new money.

CHANGING YOUR MANAGER

Some people believe that, once they have chosen an ISA manager, they are committed long-term. But this is not so. You may become unhappy with the performance, or your own needs may alter over the years. The official constraint is that, when you change, you must stay with the same component: you can only transfer from a shares and unit trust maxi ISA to another similar maxi ISA, and not to a cash mini ISA.

In the marketplace, rules vary and you need to check before making a decision. Some managers will charge a fee if you want to leave; some are happy to transfer shares, but others will insist on realising your investments and sending cash to the new manager. It generally makes sense to talk first either to an adviser or to the management group to which you want to move your money.

WEEDING AND DIVERSIFYING

The experts will tell you that there are two secrets to successful investment in ISAs – weeding out poor performers and diversifying so that you have a wide spread of assets. Checking performance twice a year is probably enough, unless your basic objectives change, say on retirement. Don't necessarily throw out last year's bad fund performer: look at the consistency of performance over a number of separate annual periods. Diversifying – don't put your eggs in one basket – is one of the basic investment rules. Your fundamental split will be between equities and bonds, but do not forget investments in commodities and commercial property. You should also consider a geographical split of your investments: as your liabilities are all in the UK, you will probably want to keep at least half your assets here. But ponder the appeal of the two major world economies, the US and Japan, along with Europe and Asia Pacific. You will, at all times, need to consider whether you take your own investment decisions, using the press and the Internet, or whether you need professional advice from an independent financial adviser (IFA). If you choose an IFA, then you will have to pay, through a fee or commission or possibly a combination of the two.

FUNDS TO COMPLEMENT YOUR ISAs

ISAs are a government creation, offering useful tax breaks, which can be low-risk or high-risk as you choose. Among the many funds that are on offer in the marketplace, three are worth considering to stand alongside your ISAs.

Roll-up funds, which defer tax, are low-risk. **Friendly Societies**, which offer a tax-free investment, are also low-risk. **Hedge funds**, which most people will have heard of, do not offer specific tax advantages, though your profit will probably come as capital gain rather than income; hedge funds are higher-risk.

ROLL-UP FUNDS

These are cash or money-market funds where interest is rolled up and reinvested as opposed to being paid out. Roll-up funds are generally low-risk, as they tend to concentrate on short-term securities issued by leading banks and other high-quality borrowers. The usual structure follows that of a unit trust, so that the shares or units can be bought and sold easily and quickly.

Roll-up finds are often listed, and generally based in a tax-friendly location such as Ireland, the Channel Islands or Luxembourg. They are sponsored by major banks and insurance companies.

Yields and charges

Before deciding whether a roll-up fund is right for you, it is a good idea to consider yields and costs. The traditional bond fund test is relevant: the higher the yield, the greater the risk. And higher-yielding funds often make higher charges.

If you are risk-averse, there are a number of roll-up funds that offer yields that are close to the Bank of England base rate and where the charges are correspondingly low – say no initial charge and 1% a year for management. These funds are invested in high-grade short-term paper (such as certificates of deposit issued by leading banks) so that their risk exposure is low. You also need to be aware whether the manager's charges are taken from capital or income.

How roll-ups work

As the fund does not pay any interest or dividends, its income is ploughed back before tax into the fund. You are therefore getting interest on interest, which gives you all the benefits of compounding. If you check the price of your units, you will see that they rise, slightly, from one day to the next.

The tax situation is important: you are not taxed when the interest on your units is ploughed back into the fund. You pay tax when you cash in, and then you are liable for income tax on the gain: if you bought the units at £1.20 each and sold for £1.50, you pay tax on the 30p.

So if you find that you do need income, then you have to sell some units – as a rule, you should get your cash within a few days.

Why choose a roll-up?

You can now see the sort of people to whom a roll-up fund will appeal:

- Investors saving for retirement who expect that their tax rate will be lower – say moving from higher rate to standard rate once they retire.

- People who are planning to retire overseas, who can defer tax payments until they move abroad.

- Investors who want to choose when and how much money they draw down and when they pay tax on their income.

- Investors who are looking for income in the medium to longer term rather than the present.

Some side-benefits

The principal side-benefit of investing in a roll-up is that you access, indirectly, the wholesale finance market, which is usually open only to the investment institutions. You may also be able to take a currency position, which could be useful either as a speculation or if you are going to live abroad. Some funds offer you the facility to switch your sterling units to another major currency free of charge or for a nominal cost – and this switch should not count as a cash-in on which you would have to pay tax. But you have to remember that you will get the rate of interest which is appropriate to that currency: at the time of writing, US short-term rates were lower than British rates so that a switch from sterling to dollars would bring a lower yield.

FRIENDLY SOCIETIES

Friendly Societies are safe, long-established, mutual finance companies which offer their members a range of savings, insurance and related products. Friendly societies are included here because they also offer the public very small-scale but tax-free products.

Everyone can take advantage of the tax-free savings allowance, which permits you to invest up to £25 a month or £270 a year free of income tax and capital gains tax. (The Societies themselves often impose a minimum of £15 a month.) Your investment runs for 10 years, so many people just hand over £2,000–£2,500, which is put into a taxable account and gradually fed into the tax-free policy.

Just like a bond

A typical Friendly Society plan will centre on a with-profit bond.

When you begin, you first decide how much you want to invest; based on that the Friendly Society will guarantee a sum assured which you will get at the end of the 10 years. Growth in your investment comes from annual bonuses – and perhaps a terminal bonus at the end. Once your annual bonuses have been added, they cannot be taken away, but they are not guaranteed and will depend on the performance of the (traditional-type) investment portfolio.

Over the past ten years, a Friendly Society bond should have done better than a building society investment. That may not seem too bad, but you have given up access to your money, and there are penalties if you stop paying premiums within the early years – you may even get back less that you had invested. For higher-rate taxpayers, a tax liability can also arise if you make the policy paid up and then surrender before the end of the term. You should recognise that this is a 10-year investment.

Bonds for the family?
A Friendly Society bond is a very small investment, but you could take out bonds for yourself, your spouse and teenage children: the normal age range is 16–70. You also get the benefit of a modest amount of life cover plus a payment into your estate if you die before the 10 years are up.

Whether your family should have a bond will depend on share prices: if stock market prices move ahead over the 10 years, you would be better off in an equity tracker. But the Friendly Societies could say that their return over 10 years of 3.6% a year compares with 2.1% from a typical building society.

But costs look high

Just because of the official limits on the size of Friendly Society investment, costs come out looking rather high. Even over a 10-year term, setting-up costs and operating expenses are relatively large: in one of the better-known Societies, the total deductions for someone investing £25 a month would amount to more than £500 over the 10 years.

Put another way – leaving out the cost of life cover – the deductions would bring down the rate of growth from an assumed 7% a year to 4.5%. That represents a fall of more than one third.

You are not likely to lose

You are very unlikely to lose your money if you invest in a bond run by a Friendly Society. You may find, at the end of the 10 years, that you could have done better, perhaps even much better. But if stock markets repeat the 50% drop of 2000–2003, plus the intervening volatility, you will have done well with a Friendly Society. You could hand over the lump sum of £2,000 plus and then forget about the bond for 10 years, at the end of which you will receive a pleasant, if small-sized, surprise.

HEDGE FUNDS

Most people have heard of hedge funds often without a clear idea of what they are or how you can invest. It was George Soros' hedge fund which helped to force the pound out of the Exchange Rate Mechanism, while a few years later another hedge fund collapsed and led to near-panic on Wall Street. World wide there are now reckoned to be around 8,000 hedge funds, mostly focusing on American investors.

The first point to emphasise is that you should invest only if you have a sizeable portfolio and if you are prepared to accept possibly large investment risks. Hedge fund managers will say that their aim is to provide absolute returns, even when markets are going down.

What is a hedge fund?

Essentially a hedge fund is a unit trust structure that employs a range of sophisticated techniques, such as selling short, to trade in a range of assets – shares, currencies, commodities. They are private investment pools. To hedge originally meant to protect yourself against a loss on a bet by placing another bet, but the hedge funds' techniques now go way beyond that basic formula.

Not in the public domain

You will not, for now, find advertisements for hedge funds because the Financial Services Authority restricts access, although a number of leading hedge fund groups are based in the UK. To find out more you will need to go through a broker or a financial adviser, unless you can persuade the hedge fund manager that you are an experienced investor.

When you do find out more, you are liable to be impressed by two features of hedge funds. One is that the minimum investment is likely to be large, though this is starting to change. The second feature is that fees are higher than with conventional unit trusts: a hedge fund manager may charge a standard 2% a year, but will generally look for a much larger fee, say 20–30% of the extent that performance exceeds some predetermined index.

Fund of funds

By all means explore the world of hedge funds – when you get their data, you will often find careful and detailed analysis. If you feel that you want to invest, think about the 'fund of hedge funds' concept, which is promoted by some banks and fund management groups. Some banks are now promoting lower-risk hedge funds, and many pension funds have put money into hedge funds.

This spreading of hedge fund risk has an obvious appeal, and the 'fund of funds' idea has been applied in a number of financial sectors. The key point to analyse is the level of charges – you need to look at both low-performance and high-performance.

Hedge fends have benefited from many investors' search for alternative investments following the equity market setback of 2000–3, and this may continue. There is also evidence that hedge funds themselves have become more cautious, diversifying their assets and keeping borrowings down.

A final question: you will need to satisfy yourself that hedge funds are not just foul-weather performers – which do well when markets are going down. You should be reasonably sure that a hedge fund will also out-perform, say, a low-cost tracker or a conventional managed fund when markets are going up.

SUMMARY

◆ An ISA is a wrapper, which guarantees nearly total tax-free status to the cash, shares or unit trusts you put inside them – ISAs are a key part of your strategy to finance a decent pension.

- You can invest up to £7,000 each tax year in a maxi ISA for shares or unit trusts.

- You and your spouse or partner are each allowed £7,000 – joint holdings are not permitted.

- Buy your ISA through a discount broker or a funds supermarket: with share growth now expected to be in single figures, the savings are significant.

- Check the withdrawal terms in case you need to cash in before retiring.

- Find out if there are any costs or penalties if you later decide you want to move to a different fund manager.

- Think about roll-up funds, which defer tax and are low-risk; Friendly Societies, which are tax-free, on a small scale, and are low-risk; and hedge funds, which offer potential capital gains and are higher-risk.

The Fifth Step – Build a Portfolio

From early 2003, a great debate raged among people looking to protect their pensions – do you buy shares or invest in property? For anyone looking ahead 10–20 years, the answer has to be: do both. One of the oldest, and wisest, sayings in investment is that you never put all your eggs in one basket. If you have strong views one way or the other, and wish to follow your beliefs, fine – but otherwise, spread your risk.

There are two issues here: how you invest and how you exploit your investment. Investing in shares, in principle, is straightforward, as is the way you realise. Property is different, and will be reviewed in the next chapter. Remember that shares, not property, can be put into a tax-free ISA, although that can include shares in real estate and building groups. However you can put commercial property into a self-invested pension plan.

SHARES VERSUS PROPERTY – HOW THE FIGURES COMPARE

What fuelled this debate was an analysis sponsored by Prudential Assurance, which found that half of people aged between 25 and 45 saw property investment as a source of retirement income. (There were also some dire warnings to house buyers about the effect of higher interest rates and rising maintenance costs on post-war building.)

It is perhaps surprising that anyone was taken aback by these views: over the three years 2000, 2001 and 2002 shares dropped by 50% – at a time when house prices showed a rather larger percentage increase. It is worth looking at the figures in more detail: over five years house prices doubled, while the typical UK pension fund showed no change. Over 10 years property again did better (142% v 60%); it is when you look over 15- and 20-year cycles that pension funds come out on top. In the five years from 2001, equity values only just kept up with inflation.

Behind these figures are different rates of volatility – an important point for you, given that you may be seeking to cash in for a pension in say 2020 or 2030. Before the 50% drop in 2000–3, shares fell 75% in 1972–74; house prices, too, fell in the 1990s but the volatility (and therefore the risk) is that much less. Anyone who bought a house at the peak of the 1980s boom will still be showing a useful gain. But if you bought technology shares in early 2000 you will have lost most of your capital – with little chance, in many cases, of recovering your money.

The long-term scene
Information on shares goes back many years, and provides much of the case for supporters of equities. From 1869 to 2002, for example, one study shows that shares gave an annualised real return of 6.2% a year. (That rate of growth would double in 12 years.) The classic Barclays study shows that equities produced a real investment return of 7.0% a year over the past 50 years and 5.0% a year from 1900 to the present (the longer period including two world wars).

House price data do not go back as far – it is the 20% plus per annum returns of recent years which have provided the contrast with shares. Maybe the answer is to look, briefly, at the logic behind the differing performance of the two types of asset.

The basic case for houses

There are two economic bases for investment in houses. One is that the supply is limited: the UK is one of the lowest producers in Europe of new housing, mainly because of planning restrictions. The second economic base for house prices is that average house prices are closely linked to employment and average earnings; so a rise in earnings should be reflected in housing values. And over recent years has come a sharp fall in interest rates, so that the cost of paying for housing has been reduced.

The house price:earnings ratio can vary – when it gets high, as it did in the late 1980s, people begin to talk about a 'bubble' in house prices. There was a widely held view, in the early 2000s, that the ratio was starting to move up rather too fast. That in turn led to a debate on whether house prices would suddenly drop or whether the rate of growth would slow down depending, crucially, on changes in interest rates.

BUILDING A PORTFOLIO

To recap: you have decided to divide your investments roughly equally between shares and property, with your target the creation of an acceptable pension. It is now time to look at building a share and bond portfolio which you can place (at least in part) in your ISA.

Your very first step – before you make any investment decision – has to be to decide whether you build up your shares and bonds by yourself, whether you get advice, or whether you hand over the investment choices to a professional.

This is a vital first step: if you choose to do it yourself, you have to be interested in finance and you must be prepared to set aside perhaps an hour each week to review your investments and decide on any changes. If you go to a professional, you will pay. To choose your helper, try to get personal recommendations; above all, rely on your personal reactions – is this someone you can work with and whose judgment you can trust? The choice is yours. (Finding an adviser is reviewed in detail later.)

EQUITIES VERSUS FIXED INTEREST

Your first investment decision is how to divide your assets between fixed interest and equities – shares, unit trusts and OEICs (which are an up-to-date version of unit trusts). There is an old Wall Street formula, which suggests that you subtract your age from 100 and that gives you the percentage you should have in equities. A 40-year-old would then split his portfolio 60:40 between equities and fixed interest – perhaps a little on the cautious side by UK standards, but each of us has to make their own judgment on growth versus risk.

Many people will hold a few shares – probably one or two 'blue-chips', which are the large international groups in oil, pharmaceuticals and telecoms. Some people may also hold smaller companies' shares, based on personal knowledge, a legacy or a share scheme set up by their employer.

But for many investors, the attractive option will be to invest through unit trusts, which give a spread of interests together with full-time professional management. Individual shares will offer greater scope – and greater risk. If you know a company that is well-run, always remember: when you buy a share, you are buying the stock market's assessment in the future. Well-run companies' shares can be regarded as expensive and fall in price, because expectations have run ahead too fast, not-so-well-run companies' shares can be reckoned cheap, out-perform the average and may even be taken over – giving shareholders an immediate benefit.

CHOOSING A UNIT TRUST

There is a massive range of unit trusts, as a glance at any newspaper's financial pages will show you. Your first rule, as ever, is to spread your risk: unit trusts offer growth or income, an international spread or focus on particular industries. And think about buying your unit trust through a discount broker or a fund supermarket: as with an ISA, you will get a reduction in the initial, and possibly also in the annual charge.

Tracker funds are one of the unit trust types you should consider. Trackers follow a market – the whole London market, the top 100 shares, the US, Europe or the Far East. These 'passive' investments offer two advantages: first, their costs are low – it is possible to buy a UK tracker with no initial charge and an annual cost of 0.5% or less (basically, they work by computer programs). In an age of low equity yields, these modest costs are attractive. Secondly, trackers simply by-pass the traditional performance tests: their performance is the market, and over the years only a minority of fund managers, research shows, out-perform the market as a whole.

Building a portfolio – an example

On his 40th birthday, Alec Coxon wins one of the top Premium Bond prizes of £1 million. Alec and his wife plan to use half the money for a bigger house and a new car. The other half will be used for investment. Alec just has his employer's final salary pension scheme. What does he do with his £500,000?

◆ He makes sure the money does not linger in his bank but moves to a higher-yielding account.

◆ He pays off all his existing debt – mortgage, credit cards, car loan.

◆ He puts aside six months' salary in a higher-yielding account for a rainy day.

◆ He sets up ISAs for himself and his wife plus a cash mini ISA for their 17-year-old – and determines to do this every financial year.

◆ He arranges a stakeholder pension for his wife, who is a 10% taxpayer.

◆ He invests 40% of the rest, around £150,000, in three different managers' bond funds; he mixes higher and lower yielding and buys them all through a discount broker.

◆ The rest, just over £200,000, will go into equities, and he starts by putting 35% of that into overseas tracker funds, 15% in the US and 10% each in Europe and the Far East.

◆ He now has around £125,000 to invest in the UK, of which half goes into two market trackers. He divides the rest between two unit trusts – high yield and growth, and he buys these through a fund supermarket.

◆ He now owns 10 unit trusts – apart from the ISAs – which he believes are sufficient to give him a wide spread of risk but not too numerous to be difficult to watch over.

PICKING THE RIGHT MANAGER

With a passive tracker, you can easily find out how it is
progressing: you know how the market has performed, and your
investment will have done the same (save only for the trust's
charges – which is why it is important you choose a low-cost
fund).

There is a contrary view – that you should look for a good
investment group or a skilful manager, and follow them. And in
some sectors, such as high yield trusts and aggressive choice funds,
the results have emerged ahead of the average. This is a good
theory, which can work – provided you have the time and energy to
keep a close watch on your investment. Fund managers are human,
and can change jobs and they retire – they can falter after several
years of successful out-performance. Some funds (especially in the
US) have run out of steam once they pass a certain size. You will
also pay more for a managed fund than for a tracker, so be sure
that you are getting value for money,

IMPORTANCE OF A WIDE SPREAD

One group of unit trusts you should consider are those offering
exposure to world markets outside the UK. A US or continental
tracker has obvious appeal, and you can find unit trusts which
specialise in the Far East, including or excluding Japan. The
greater part of your investments will be in the UK, on the old-
established financial principle that your assets should match your
liabilities. But spreading your risk is almost always a good idea,
and it is a fact that over the past 10 years both the US
(significantly) and continental Europe (slightly) have out-
performed the UK.

What makes markets move?

If you decide to manage your own portfolio, you will need some guidelines to succeed. And if you hand over to an outsider, you need to keep yourself informed – to know what questions to ask and the better to understand the answers.

Here are ten factors that influence the markets:

◆ **Interest rates**: set every Thursday by the Bank of England, which has an obligation to keep price inflation at 2.5% a year. A cut in interest rates should help expansion by lowering the cost of borrowing, while a rise equals a touch on the brakes.

◆ **Level of the pound**: a lower pound helps UK exporters, though it will add to inflation as imports will cost more – a key pointer is whether a change is planned or dictated by the market.

◆ **Retail trade figures**: a key indicator of consumer demand, although they can be affected by the weather and public holidays.

◆ **Earnings and unemployment**: two danger signs are a rise in unemployment, which points to a fall in demand, and a surge in earnings, which may lead to counter-action by the Bank of England.

◆ **Retail prices**: changes are your guide to inflation – you need to take action if inflation falls well below 2.5% (potential recession) or goes well above (bad news for fixed incomes).

◆ **Industrial output**: a slower rate of growth may point to recession or falling exports, caused by overseas recession or too high a level for the pound.

◆ **Wall Street**: the biggest stock market in the world, with an important impact on the UK – it may move for domestic reasons, but you need to be aware how it is performing.

◆ **Company results**: even if you don't hold the shares, watch to see whether companies' results are emerging better or worse than analysts expected – and why.

◆ **Property prices**: you may not go out and invest in property, but the value of your own home will be affected, and if prices go on rising the Bank of England may raise interest rates.

◆ **Taxation**: don't let tax drive your decisions, but tax changes can affect your investments.

These differences may continue: Gordon Brown's £5 billion a year tax on dividends was, and remains, a huge blow to UK pension funds. But the tax has had other long-term effects: it has reduced pension funds' appetite for ordinary shares, for which they are traditionally important buyers, and pushed them towards bonds, where they can still reclaim tax. Some people believe that this tax helps to explain the under-performance of the UK market against the US and the Continent; if they are right, that under-performance may continue.

TWO FURTHER THOUGHTS

An equity portfolio consisting of some shares and a number of unit trusts represents a sound base for progress. But there are two further investments you could consider as your equities begin to perform. One is investment trusts, which in effect are listed companies that invest in other listed companies. There are several hundred investment trusts on the London stock market, some holding general portfolios, others specialising in sectors such as real estate or geographic areas. Compared with unit trusts, investments trusts often sell at a small discount to the value of their total assets, and they can borrow, which should improve their shares' performance.

One other possible investment area is the Alternative Investment Market (AIM), whose rules allow listing for smaller companies than the main London exchange, often with shorter records. Many shares on AIM are relatively high-risk, but AIM also includes some large and successful companies. Part of AIM's appeal is that it offers useful tax advantages, on both inheritance tax and capital gains tax – after two years, a higher rate taxpayer would pay only 10% on capital gains made from selling AIM shares. It is always, correctly, said that you should never invest for tax reasons. But if you like to pick ordinary shares, this is a market worth remembering.

How to give away shares – an example

Peter Tallon has two small shareholdings, one ordinary shares the other zero dividend preferences, which he plans to give away to charity. He has a profit on the ordinary shares but a loss on the zero preferences.

He plans simply to hand over both holdings but the charity Treasurer, who is an old friend, points out that he could arrange things better.

It makes sense to give away the ordinary shares, so that he has no tax to pay on his gain, but if he gave away the zero preferences he would lose the capital loss which he can use to set against other profits to carry forward.

So he sells the zero preferences on the stock market and gives the money to the charity through Gift Aid. In this way he gets to keep the capital loss which may be useful later, and the charity gets its money which it can boost by 28% in the usual way.

BUYING FIXED INTEREST

If you follow the Wall Street rule (60:40 equities to fixed interest for a 40-year old), fixed interest investment will form a steadily growing part of your portfolio.

Bond unit trusts

Many people buy their fixed interest through a bond unit trust –
as already noted, this is especially suited to an ISA as the
manager can reclaim the 20% tax deducted from the interest
payments.

There is now a range of corporate bond funds from which you
can choose: the basic rule of thumb is that the higher the yield,
the greater the risk. At the time of writing, a bond fund that kept
to high-quality investments would yield 4–5%, but other funds
would give 7–8%, putting some of their money into lower-rated
issues. As always, spread your risk: if you hold some lower-
yielding funds, then think about a riskier investment. If you are by
nature risk-averse, stay with the safer lower-yielding funds.

Individual company bonds

There is an alternative to a bond fund: you can buy a company
bond through the stock market. The problem for a private
investor is that these bonds tend to be traded in large amounts. A
major risk is that you are putting your money into a single
company, as opposed to the spread you will receive through a
bond fund. Even big household-name companies can run into
difficulties, which can down-grade their bonds.

Against this, there is an advantage in buying a bond, that you
have a final redemption date which will protect your capital value
as maturity approaches. In a bond fund, your capital value
depends on the market. But buying bonds, rather than bond
funds, is essentially for larger and more sophisticated investors.

RISKIER IDEAS – WITH TAX BREAKS

If you have the appetite for greater investment risk, and can use concessions on income tax and capital gains tax, you have two possibilities: the Enterprise Investment Scheme (EIS) and Venture Capital Trusts.

EIS aims to channel money (minimum £500) into unquoted trading companies – unquoted including the Alternative Investment Market. You can now invest up to £400,000 each tax year; provided you hold the shares for at least three years, you will get 20% relief on income tax and you can defer capital gains tax on any asset within a four-year time frame of making your EIS investment. You should not have any connection with the company in which you invest.

Venture Capital Trusts are effectively pooled EIS investments, offering income tax relief on up to £200,000 worth of shares issued since April 2006 (40% relief for two years from April 2004). But the Chancellor has tightened the qualifying tests: a VCT investor will now need to hold his shares for five, not three, years if he wants to retain his tax benefits. And the gross asset limits for qualifying companies have been halved, arguably increasing the investment risk.

NUTS AND BOLTS – KEEPING RECORDS

You are building your portfolio in order to be able to afford a decent pension; this means that you have to operate a record and filing system. This system has two purposes – to satisfy the Inland Revenue and to give you the data you need for portfolio management.

You will already have a filing system for tax – an especially detailed one if you are self-employed. The law requires you to keep records for up to six years; if you are self-employed there is the chance of an Inland Revenue inquiry when your record-keeping would come under scrutiny. You also need records to protect yourself: the Inland Revenue can make mistakes, not always in your favour.

ISAs

For ISAs, record-keeping is relatively simple: you do not need to tell the taxman when you buy or sell an ISA or what income you receive. You should keep records as a guide to your total asset position (you should receive the manager's report every six months) and for your estate. But the main purpose of ISA records is for you to monitor performance: you may want to change managers if an ISA is performing badly and you also need to be aware if an ISA performs unusually well – a problem you might like to have, but one that could change the balance of your portfolio.

Shares and dividends

Outside an ISA, the record-keeping becomes rather more complex. When you buy shares or units, you need to log the total amount you paid, including the broker's commission and stamp duty, and the date (essential for calculating your capital gain when you come to sell). You also need to record any subsequent scrip issues together with any rights issues.

Nowadays you may not receive a share certificate – electronics are taking over – so you need to keep the contract note which gives details of your purchase. You will also need to note the address of the company, which will appear in the accounts and half-yearly statements which are sent to you, and note in particular the name and address of the registrars.

For future gains tax, it is important to record which shares are held by you, which by your spouse and which are owned jointly – to use two sets of tax allowances.

Keeping a log

You will keep a log of dividends for tax purposes: the net amount received, the tax credit and the date. Many people have their dividends mandated to their bank account, which saves time and cost compared with receiving a dividend cheque and sending it to your bank. In this imperfect world, you need to check from time to time that the dividends are reaching your account when they should.

Companies and unit trusts can merge with others or just change their names. You need to keep this on file, partly for your own guidance in later years and partly for the Inland Revenue, who may think you are selling a share they were not aware you had ever bought!

SUMMARY

- For long-term growth to fund your pension, you need to invest in property -- including your own home – together with shares or unit trusts.

- In shares or unit trusts, you need a mix of fixed interest and equity investments.

- Under a Wall Street formula, your age equals the percentage you hold in fixed interest.

◆ Trackers are worth considering among unit trusts – these are low-cost funds that simply mirror a particular market.

◆ Consider whether you want to run your own portfolio of long-term assets or whether you prefer to pay for outside advice; if you opt for DIY, you need to set aside the time, buy the right newspapers and use the Internet.

◆ Have some international exposure: the US stock market has out-performed London over recent years.

◆ The Alternative Investment Market is relatively risky, but offers tax attractions.

◆ For fixed interest investment, bond funds spread your risk – though a single bond offers a redemption date.

◆ It is essential to keep files and records – for the sake of the Inland Revenue, your heirs, and above all, yourself.

PROTECTED INVESTMENTS – HAVE YOUR CAKE AND EAT IT?

Some people, when advised to buy ordinary shares to help towards a decent pension, will point to their shattering experiences of 2000–3, when they lost half their capital. If only, they say, there was some way to share in equities' growth and yet keep your capital intact.

There is a way to have your cake and eat it – protected investments. These offer you a share in the growth of equities over, say, a five- or six-year period and the guarantee that you will get your capital back, whatever has happened to share prices, at the end of the period. In return for your money-back guarantee you give up flexibility and access, while any profit may come as income rather than capital. These plans will appeal to the very cautious or the very bruised.

Precipice bonds are different

The crucial test for all of these plans is the guarantee that you get all your money back. Over the years, investors have put money into so-called precipice bonds, which return your original investment only if a share index or group of shares has maintained its value. These bonds' time-span may be relatively short, sometimes three years, and their great attraction is that they offer high yields – possibly around 10% a year – which can be taken as either income or capital growth.

Your capital in these cases is not guaranteed, but only conditionally guaranteed. If the share indices fall far enough (the indices chosen were often London, Eurostoxx or the Nasdaq index of technology shares in the US) then you could lose all of your capital. Investors bought these bonds, attracted by the high returns, shortly before the stock market crash of 2000–3; some got their money back but others faced losses anywhere between 20% and 100% – partly offset by the 30% or so income/capital they had received over the years.

Precipice bonds are still being sold; they have a useful investment role, provided you appreciate exactly what you are buying. Essentially, these bonds are a way of speculating on the future of the stock market – that over the succeeding years the market will rise, or at the very least that it will not fall.

A typical current product will offer you double any growth in the London market over, say, five years, capped at 50%. If the index falls over this period, then your capital will be reduced by 1% by every 1% fall in the index, with the maximum reduction set at 15%.

You have a stop-loss in place, which limits your risk, in return for accepting a limit on your share in the growth.

In a more sophisticated version, funds are revalued every quarter and a limit is set on how far investors' funds can fall. The objective is to ratchet up the value of the fund when the stock market is rising and limit the losses when the market is going down.

If this sort of investment appeals to you, you need to compare 'erosion' levels: an investment where the index has to fall 50% before your capital is eroded is better than one where the trigger is 30%.

Keeping your capital safe

The very cautious, who want to limit the risks on their pension assets and be sure to keep their money capital, will prefer a guaranteed plan which could be a six-year scheme, offering up to 125% of the growth in share prices. At the end of that period, you get your money back, so that if share prices fall over the period you have missed out on interest and dividends, while your money capital is worth less in real terms.

But not more than 25 to 30% of your portfolio

Even if you are cautious, a general view is that you should not put more than 25 to 30% of your portfolio into protected products – principally because you are temporarily giving up control of your capital.

Your first question centres on the guarantee. National Savings have offered a similar product, in which case your guarantee comes from the government.

If you invest in a plan from one of the major banks or insurance companies, then your guarantee is as good as that company and the others which are helping to arrange the operation. (The bank or insurance company from which you buy the plan will enter into complex financial arrangements to meet its commitment to you.)

A five-year wait

A fully protected plan will generally run for five to six years. One important point to note is that you will not be able to access your money during this time – maybe not at all or under a penalty which you may not be able to forecast. (ISA investments have to be listed so in those cases you will in theory be able to sell, but access to market deals can vary between limited and practically non-existent.) Your gain, as with National Savings, may come as income rather than capital.

The second point you need to recognise is that you will not receive any interest or dividends during the five years: some plans allow you to nominate a 5% annual income, but this will be at the expense of your capital guarantee. A dividend/interest sacrifice over five years will represent a significant opportunity cost.

Late fluctuations

There is an obvious issue on timing you need to consider: if you took out a five-year plan in June 2006, you are looking at the state of the market in June 2011. Plan sponsors will often look at the average value of the market during the last six months or year of the plan; this will help reduce anomalies, but not get rid of them.

Imagine a situation where the market starts a steady rise after you invest, peaks in year three and then goes into steady decline. You might not have much of a profit to show at the end of five years. If you had held your own investments you might have sold in year three and gone back into the market after year five.

Variations on a theme

Some plan sponsors have devised interesting variations to counter these issues. In one six-year plan, there is a review after year 3: if the market has risen 21%, the plan is wound up and you get back your initial stake plus the 21%. The same exercise is repeated after five years, if the market has risen by 55%. If the plan survives both these tests, it runs for the full six years, and you get back all of the growth in the market. The end-year six value is taken as the average level of the market for the final year.

Sacrifice of potential growth

Protected products have been improved over recent years. The size of your possible loss has been reduced and the product range has been widened – to include, for example, growth in house prices. Explanations, too, are much clearer; this matters, because banks and insurance companies are likely to resist paying compensation if the risks were clearly explained.

The bottom line has to be: if you are cautious, go for a protected product but limit the extent of your investment.

SUMMARY

◆ Protection plans guarantee that you will get back your initial capital – in return you sacrifice flexibility and access.

◆ These plans, promoted by leading banks and insurance companies, typically run for five or six years.

◆ Some of these plans can be placed in an ISA (when the shares have a European listing), so that any final surplus will be free of tax.

◆ Check on how share price performance will be measured – such as the average of 6 or 12 months before the plan matures.

◆ It is important to distinguish protection plans from precipice bonds, where you get your capital back only so long as certain defined indexes or share prices do not fall – or do not fall by very much.

◆ Protection plans should be regarded as part-equity investments – and probably represent not more than 25–30% of your total portfolio.

CUTTING THE COST OF KIDS

To rear and educate a child now costs, it is estimated, around £300,000 on average – and you could spend more if you choose private education, leading to one of the major boarding schools. Expenditure at this rate could cut back your pension assets, while saving on your children could be a great help. It is important to remember:

◆ there is a range of attractive investment products which are designed specifically for children

◆ children have their own tax allowances which you can put to good use – something which too few people exploit.

High street and savings accounts

A starting-point has to be the savings and deposit accounts for children, which tend to offer better rates than those for adults. Assuming that the child's interest income will be less than its personal allowance (£5,035 for 2006–7) you can arrange to have interest paid gross and it will all be tax-free!

The familiar snag is that the Inland Revenue insists that if the child's money comes from a parent, then it will be taxed as the parent's once the total goes over £100 a year.

There are two possible solutions:

(a) invest the child's assets in tax-free products: National Savings certificates, or you could buy premium bonds, and/or

(b) arrange for the money to come from grandparents, godparents or friends and make sure that the source is well documented.

How to buy shares for children

If you are building a portfolio for children, you will probably buy some fixed-rate bonds just because the effective tax-free return is so appealing. But if you are taking a 10-year perspective, or longer, then you should be looking at equities – investment trusts, tracker funds or well-performing unit trusts. If you look over the maximum 18 years, an average investment trust (on past results) could grow your initial capital six- to sevenfold and the most successful by far more.

You may need advice on the procedures to follow when you buy shares for your kids. This can be done in two ways:

- **Designate**: you designate the account with the child's initials. That has the appeal of simplicity; you can access the investment if, for instance, you need money to pay school fees. The bad news is that a designated account remains your money, so that you are liable for tax.

- **Bare trust**: this can be simply arranged, and means that the money is regarded as the child's own. (If the amount is large, look out for the tax liabilities created by the 2006 budget.) You can still change investments within the trust, but you need to take care: if you have a prior obligation to pay school fees and use the bare trust, it could be argued that you are benefiting, which would be a breach of trust. Finally, when the child reaches age 18, the trust is dissolved and the child takes the money.

Because the money is the child's own, its allowances apply: £5,035 on income and £8,800 on capital gains for 2006–7. These give tax-free income and represent a useful way to shelter family assets.

(Note: children reach the age of legal maturity at 18 in England but 16 in Scotland; there are also differences in trust arrangements which you need to recognise if the donors are Scottish residents.)

A Child Trust Fund – from the government

The government have now weighed in with a Child Trust Fund: every child born after September 2002 will get £250 paid into a new account, or £500 if the family qualifies for full child tax credit. The government will add a further amount when the child reaches seven, and possibly at a later stage, while family and friends will be able to contribute up to £1,200 a year. The child will not be able to touch the fund until age 18, but will then be free to use the money however it chooses.

The scheme did not start until 2005, with payments backdated. The stakeholder version will be managed on a 'lifestyle' basis – gradually switched into cash and fixed interest during the last five years to age 18. Charges are set at 1.5% – potential suppliers have been urging an increase on the initial stakeholder 1% – too little, they say, for effective advice and marketing. Even so, some leading names of suppliers are missing.

Two investment options – Friendly Societies and stakeholder pensions

There are other options for grandparents or other donors who want to help. One is to use a Friendly Society, where the investment will be unit-linked or with-profits. As the section on Friendly Societies shows (Chapter 4), their principal drawback is the relatively high level of charges. Some Societies have taken this issue on board and offer more appealing terms for child savers, such as waiving the initial charge or policy fee and keeping the annual management charge to 1%. Friendly Societies' other drawback remains that investment is limited to £270 a year or £25 a month.

Some people are bothered by the structure of a bare trust and the Child Trust Fund: that at age 18 the new adult can take the money and spend it however they choose – maybe in ways that have nothing to do with their education! For cautious people with these concerns, a second investment option would be to set up a stakeholder pension. It is only a few years ago that it became possible to invest in a pension for a child, and the stakeholder is tax-efficient. The basic payment of £3,600 a year costs £2,808, with the government paying the extra £792.

The problem is that the child will not be able to access the stakeholder pension until they reach age 55, which rules it out as a way to help pay for education. But if your primary aim is to pass on capital, you could set up a stakeholder pension for, say, the first five years of the child's life. The premiums could be invested in a tracker fund; if you assume growth at 5% a year, the child could look forward to a six-figure pension fund at retirement, producing an annuity income of several thousand pounds a year at today's prices.

This may be long-term planning carried to extreme, but in the time to come today's child may bless the donor of former years – plus the power of compound interest!

Make sure they take a student loan

Many kids, when they get to college, will use student loans to cover their living costs. But even if your kids can manage without the money, make sure that they take the loan and invest: at the end of their three years, they should be several hundred pounds better off.

The basis for this advice is that a student pays significantly less interest on a student loan than they can get by investing. At the time of writing, an instant access account offered about 2% more than the cost of a student loan. Everyone can claim 75% of the student loan maximum, as set by the government. Repayment has to begin the April after graduation, as long as the graduate is earning over £15,000 a year.

Tax should not be an issue: unless earnings go over £5,035 a year (for 2006–7) the student will not have to pay tax on their savings and will be entitled to receive interest gross. If a student does pay tax, the investment should go into a cash mini ISA, where the rates tend to be at or slightly above instant access. Anyone over 16 can put £3,000 into a cash mini ISA in each tax year.

Hitting the givers – an example

Julian and Anne Harvey transferred ownership of their house to their daughter just seven years ago. They are happy that now the property is no longer considered part of their estate and so will not form part of the assets on which Inheritance Tax is calculated.

But Julian and Anne have not been paying their daughter any rent, so the Inland Revenue wants this to be taxed – in the eyes of the government they have been getting a benefit in kind.

The government is going to use the official rate of interest – 5% at present – to work out the supposed market rent on which tax will be charged.

Their house is worth £200,000, so the market rent is assessed at £10,000. Julian and Anne pay tax on this amount: as they pay tax at the standard rate of 22%, they will have to pay £2,200 a year. If they had been higher rate taxpayers, the bill would have been £4,000.

Equity release has been exempted from these rules, so Julian and Anne wish, with hindsight, that they had taken a lifetime mortgage seven years ago. They could have given the money to their daughter and after seven years their gift would have escaped Inheritance Tax. And the lifetime mortgage, as a debt, would have reduced the value of their estate. They feel they have suffered because the government has back-dated the new rules.

NATIONAL SAVINGS – ABOUT AS SAFE AS YOU CAN GET

National Savings are guaranteed by Her Majesty's Government, which in the UK is about as safe as you can get. Over recent years Russia and Argentina have defaulted, but this country's record stays impeccable.

As an investor, you pay for this impeccable record: the returns you get are lower than those offered by leading banks and insurance companies. So for all their wide range of products and massive support (perhaps half the entire population), National Savings offer a relatively limited range as you build up the assets which will buy you an acceptable pension – with one exception, premium bonds.

So you want to be a millionaire?

If you want to become a millionaire, you can play the lottery, though the odds are long. You can try for a place on the TV programme. Or you can decide that you will invest £100 a month in the stock market; if your funds earn 12.5% a year, which is better than shares have averaged over the last 50 years, then at the end of a 40-year working life you will have amassed £1 million. Or you can buy premium bonds.

You can buy up to £30,000 worth of premium bonds, on which since October 2004 you have been paid 3.2% free of tax – which means that Premium Bonds are mainly of interest to higher rate

Trusts – The 2006 Budget Attack

The March 2006 Budget clamped down on trusts; later, the tough new rules were partly eased. Result: picture still far from clear. Two trust types were targeted:

Accumulation and Maintenance (A&M): previously, income had to be paid out to the beneficiary by age 25; no rules about capital. Now, capital has also to be paid out by age 25 with a charge of 0.6% a year from age 18. You can no longer put assets into an A&M trust in your lifetime and avoid an immediate IHT charge – anything above the IHT limit of £285,000 (for 2006–7) will be hit by a one-off 20% charge.

Life interest: also known as Interest in Possession (IIP) where the Chancellor back-tracked: couples can still put assets into IIP trusts free of tax for the eventual benefit of the children with a lifetime interest for the surviving spouse. But lifetime transfers into an IIP trust will now be charged on the same basis as A&M trusts.

Insurance policies: written in trust have been widely used, e.g. to arrange cover for future IHT costs on the family. Deals done before March 22 will be safe; there will be no retrospective levy. But there will be a new charge; policies will only escape if no more than £285,000 is paid in over seven years.

You still have some time to reflect and seek advice. Transitional provisions are in place to give people affected the opportunity to unravel what they had planned. These provision are in place until April 2008.

One type of trust seems to have escaped the Chancellor's eagle eye – **discretionary will trusts** which save IHT. First step is for a husband and wife to own their houses as tenants in common; when the first spouse dies, assets up to the nil rate band (£285,000) go to a discretionary trust for the couple's children. The survivor gives the trust an IOU for the £285,000; on the second death the trust calls in the loan, which comes off the value of the survivor's estate. IHT saving: up to £114,000.

taxpayers. (Your spouse or partner can buy the same amount.) This interest is paid into a fund, from which there are drawings every month – more than 700,000 lucky people. If you enjoy average luck, you should get a prize every month if you hold the maximum. The drawings are made by ERNIE, who is a machine, and the random nature of his decisions is verified by the Government Actuary.

More than 90% of these premium bond prizes are in the smallest category, £50 or £100, but for the past 10 years there has been one each month of £1 million – now increased to two a month – so that National Savings have created more than 100 millionaires. Nowadays, £1 million represents around 40 times the average wage and would if invested give a higher-rate taxpayer £30,000 net a year.

Premium bonds are a lottery, but here you are gambling only with the interest: your money capital is safe. How much you want to gamble this way has to be a question only you can answer. There is clearly an appeal in buying the minimum £100 of premium bonds, which will give you the chance of a prize – though the chance will be a very small one. Your £100 buys you 100 separate bonds, all with an equal chance of winning. At the other extreme, people who can afford it may go for the maximum £30,000 and wait to see how good their luck proves to be. All prizes are free of tax and do not even have to be reported to the Inland Revenue.

Premium bonds are liquid: if you decide your luck is worse than average, you should be able to cash in after seven working days. And there is no time limit on prizes: amazingly, there is more than £20 million outstanding in unclaimed prizes. National

Savings will write to you, and you can always check through their website.

Certificates for the short term

National Savings certificates are worth monitoring, for their rates can occasionally become attractive when set against commercial products. (Cynics point out that this tends to happen when rates are falling, when National Savings tend to be rather slow to catch up.)

Certificates come in two sorts, **fixed-rate** and **index-linked**, and in two periods, two-year and five-year for the fixed-rate and three-year and five-year for index-linked. They are tax-free, but with relatively low rates so that they will appeal primarily to higher-rate taxpayers: standard rate payers would do better in the commercial market; so would lower-rate and non-taxpayers.

Index-linked certificates pay a small premium over inflation, slightly more for the five-year issue than for the three-year. For a higher-rate taxpayer prepared to lock up your money for three years, the rate has some attraction: you get a 0.7% premium over inflation, so if inflation averages 3% you get 3.7% net which is worth an appealing 6.2% gross if you pay 40% tax. You can hold up to £10,000 in each issue, so can your spouse. The fixed-rate issue, especially the two year product, may offer you opportunities from time to time – but remember that if you have to cash in early, you will get no interest for the first year. You should compare the rate on these certificates with two-year fixed deposits and bonds in the market. Do not rush in if you think interest rates generally are on the rise.

A protected investment

National Savings may be of limited value in helping you afford a decent pension, but they remain popular because they are easy to buy – you can simply walk into a post office – and because they are safe.

To keep up with the market, National Savings have launched a protected investment – a guaranteed equity bond – and issue 6 offered to hand back 95% of the rise in the market, with no risk to your capital. That proportion represents an improvement over other recent schemes, but the drawbacks remain.

First, you have to tie up your money for five years – and you receive no dividends or interest during that time. Second, the gain comes as income, rather than capital, so that all of the profit from 95% of a boost in the market will have to appear in your annual return and be taxed at your highest rate. Thirdly, the scope for price anomalies remains, and the key level of the index will be assessed over the relatively short period of six months prior to repayment.

SUMMARY

♦ Buy the minimum of £100 of premium bonds just for the (small) chance that you will win a prize.

♦ Whatever you win on a premium bond will be tax-free, but the interest rate is relatively low.

♦ If you are prepared to gamble with your interest (your money capital is safe), and can afford the outlay, you can invest up to £30,000 – so can your spouse.

- The maximum £30,000 should give you a prize a month (over 90% of the prizes are £50) so long as you enjoy average good luck.

- If you invest the maximum, give it a year to see if your luck is average – if not, cash in.

- A protected product from National Savings offered 95% of the rise in shares over five years – but no dividends in the interim, any gain as income, and only six months before maturity in which to measure share prices.

GILT-EDGED – THE GOVERNMENT'S STOCK

Our grandparents probably placed a large part of their savings into government stocks, better known as gilt-edged. For us now, they are of limited interest – especially against the option of corporate bond funds.

Gilts, like National Savings, have the great appeal of being safe, so long as you fully appreciate what it is that you are being promised. Gilts represent a form of national savings: they are borrowings by successive governments, in the form of bonds which are listed on the stock market and are easy and cheap to trade. In this way, governments can also tap into world financial markets in order to help fund a shortfall between what they spend and what they raise in taxation.

How gilts work

When a gilt is issued, it will carry a fixed rate of interest (also known as the coupon) and a predetermined repayment date, or maybe a spread of dates. A spread means that the government must repay by the later date, but has the option to repay from the earlier date. Interest is usually paid twice a year, half the total each time.

Investors used to buy gilts to represent the fixed interest element in their portfolio – in the days when buying equities was an unusual and minority activity.

Corporate bonds yield rather more than gilts because a company, even a large one, is regarded as more of a risk than the government. Nowadays, that is considered academic, with little risk of a major company facing collapse (though don't forget Enron).

Busier market to come?

For a number of years – thanks partly to rising taxes – governments have not had to enter the bond market, but the signs are that this may be about to change as budget deficits increase. If this happens, there are two sorts of gilts you should look out for:

◆ **Low-coupon gilts** which have an early repayment date and which are being sold at a discount. Profits you make from selling gilts are free from gains tax so that the net return, especially to a higher-rate taxpayer, can be attractive – while the early repayment date acts as a support under the share price.

◆ **High-coupon gilts** which stand below their repayment amount; you get an attractive return, while the discount to repayment means that you are safe against capital loss if you hold to maturity. (Gains on gilts are free from tax – but for that reason losses from the sale of gilts are not allowable.)

Comparing gilt-edged yields

If you consider gilt-edged, you will see that two sets of yields are shown, as for bond funds – the **flat or current yield** and the **redemption yield**. The flat yield represents the money you currently receive: if you buy a 5% gilt at £100 (par value) then your flat yield is 5%. If you have to pay £125 then your return comes down to 4%; the flat yield shows the current return on your money.

The redemption yield tells you what you will get if you hold your investment until the end of its life. (A few gilt-edged, such as War Loan, are undated.) If you had bought your 5% gilt at £90, you would receive the running yield plus a £10 surplus when the stock was repaid; the redemption yield allows for that.

Conversely, on the stock that you bought for £125 you would face a £25 loss when it is repaid, and you need to offset this loss against the running yield.

Where the redemption yield stands above the running yield, you can infer that there will be a profit when the stock matures. When the redemption yield is lower, you know that there will be a loss – always assuming that you hold the stock to the end of its life.

Index-linked gilts

In the years that followed the Second World War, the value of gilts was decimated by inflation – many individuals who thought they had made a safe investment decision found their savings virtually annihilated. So the government introduced index-linked gilts, which are quoted on the stock market and available alongside index-linked saving certificates.

While many people have bought index-linked certificates, index-linked gilts have been bought mainly by pension funds and some insurance companies' specialist funds. In an index-linked gilt the interest is paid twice a year and is adjusted in line with inflation. Your capital is also re-valued every six months.

Tax treatment is the same as for the rest of the gilt market – you have to pay income tax on the interest but any capital gains are tax-free. And, like other gilts, the index-linked are cheap and easy to buy: you pay no fees, no commission is paid to advisers and stockbrokers – all you need to do is contact the Bank of England.

Low inflation has largely killed interest in index-linked gilts. Some unit trusts have been created specialising in index-linked gilts but these have been aimed mainly at pension funds. This is a market best left to the professionals: individual investors always have the option of three- or five-year index-linked certificates.

Commercial rates – minus

Gilts in many ways resemble national savings – you are offered a wide choice of assets but on terms that are generally less appealing than those in the marketplace. In other words, you are paying a significant price for the assurance of a government guarantee as compared with one from a bank or large industrial company.

Some organisations have an obligation to buy gilts rather than corporate bonds, which helps the market; an individual determined to buy or sell gilts can do so cheaply and easily via the Bank of England. But remember that you can also make losses on gilts: a gilt, like any other bond, will fall in price when interest rates rise. If the repayment date is some years away, you could show a loss on your original investment for some time until the repayment support starts to work.

It's worth keeping watch on developments in the gilt market – especially if the forecasters are right, and the government will have to find buyers for bonds over the next few years. But until some attractive products emerge, corporate bond funds will do most jobs rather better.

The Sixth Step – A Pension from Property

You have built up a portfolio of ISAs, you have some holdings of unit trusts and you contribute towards your employer's pension scheme: as you tell your friends, two of these plans are particularly tax-efficient ways to build your pension assets. But you are one of those people who see property as being a major contributor towards your pension. (A large number of people in the under 50 age bracket agree with you.) So you first think of your own home: you and your spouse decide to borrow as much as you can, buy the most expensive house you can afford and improve it as your income permits.

HOW DO YOU CASH IN?

You have taken the decision that your own home will provide a part of your pension – but how do you arrange that? Yours ISAs and unit trusts are straightforward: as stated already, you invest them into a pension plan, get the tax relief and cash in 25% of the pension that results – showing you a handsome return on your money. But how do you get the money out of your house? You need to review the possibilities before you make the decision!

Trading down

The first classic answer, which still applies in many cases, is that you trade down. Your children have left home, so you sell and buy a smaller house to suit you and your spouse. Your capital gain, which one hopes will have grown large, is free of tax (from your principal residence) and you are left with a cash surplus from the transaction to help buy a pension. As house prices have risen, many people have established equity in their house, i.e. value over and above any mortgage debt.

But this will not work in all cases: you may not want to leave the home in which you have invested so much; it may not prove easy to sell; you may find it difficult to locate the right smaller house.

Increasing your borrowing

Your first response in this situation is to borrow. At the time of writing, you could, depending on age and other conditions, take out a mortgage, put the money into a level annuity and show a surplus.

If you do take out a mortgage, it should probably be interest-only. This reduces the outflow on your resources as you don't have to set aside money to pay off what you have borrowed: the arrangement would be that the house would be sold, and the mortgage repaid, when you and your spouse have both died or gone into long-term care. That would mean that the house would not pass on to your children – unless they could pay off your debt out of their own resources or re-mortgage if they wanted to keep your home in the family.

HOW GOOD AN INVESTMENT?

At this stage, you need to form some detailed opinion of just how good an investment your house is likely to be. The general features of the UK housing market were reviewed in the last chapter on establishing your portfolio; you now need to focus on the specifics. When you go to analyse history, you face the immediate problem that house price data in this country goes back only 30 years. Over those years, you find that house price growth averaged just under 9% a year. That is less than the stock market returned – around 14% with dividends ploughed back – but there is a crucial difference, that house prices were much less volatile.

If you look back to the last 10 years or so, stock markets produced average annual growth of 10%. But within that period was the bear market of 2000–2003, when shares dropped by 50%.

How volatile are house prices?

You accept that shares represent a good long-term investment but have been volatile short-term. (Which means that, as you approach retirement, you should gradually move from equities into fixed interest – this is the 'lifestyle' plan which insurance companies will follow for you.)

If you break these past 30 years into 20 over-lapping periods of 10 years, you get the impressive result that house prices did not fall, though the rate of growth varied between under 5% to near 15%. In other words, you were certain, during these years, to see house prices recover if you were prepared to wait.

House price recessions may be short, but they can be sharp, as in the years which followed the late 1980s: in the three years between 1989 and 1992 house prices dropped nearly 20%.

Can you forecast?

If your house is important for your pension, timing – for example, when you sell to move to a smaller home – is crucial. Traditionally, there are two pointers to likely changes in house prices:

- **Income levels**. For the past 20 years, the average house sold for 3.7 times the average income. Just before the house price setback of the early 1990s, houses were selling at 5.0 times the average wage: by the early 2000s the ratio had climbed back to 4.8, which led to an outburst of warnings. The market is still helped by the expansion of equity release, the growth of buy-to-let and historically low rates of interest, though the growth in house prices has now slowed.

- **Mortgage costs**. As virtually everyone buys their house on a mortgage, house prices will be affected by how much of their income the average homeowner has to pay to the lender. In the early 1990s, the average homeowner paid around 22% of their wage on the mortgage. Now, the comparable proportion is about 15%, indicating that houses have become relatively cheaper.

LET-TO-BUY

Recent years' rise in property values, and the growth of the house rental market, have created a new way to exploit the money in your house: let-to-buy. People now understand buy-to-let, where you buy a property with the aim of letting it out as an investment – this is discussed in the next section. Let-to-buy is where you move from your own house to a smaller one, but you let your house rather than sell it.

This strategy depends on rising house prices and low mortgage rates. Instead of using sale proceeds, you borrow on a mortgage – when rates are historically low – to buy your new smaller house.

The rent from your let more than covers the mortgage interest on your new house – you need a reasonable margin, because your rental income is taxable, while you pay mortgage interest net. But you are still the owner of your original house; you own the two houses, giving you a significant stake in property, and you feel confident that the future rise in house prices will pay off the mortgage you have taken out.

You are always free to change your strategy and sell your original house if your needs change or if you believe that house prices have peaked (though as it's no longer your principal residence, your gain will be taxable). There is also the assumption that your original house can be easily let, at an appealing percentage of its capital value.

EQUITY RELEASE

You might be considering equity release – the name describes what you want, and you will have read that hundreds of millions of pounds have been raised this way. For many people, equity release may be the only way to achieve an acceptable living standard in retirement. Before you explore the three main ways of arranging equity release, two words of caution need to be set out:

◆ The amount you will be able to borrow will be less than the value of your house; depending on your age and the type of scheme you select, the cash you get will be between 25% and 40% of its market value.

◆ Though equity release is offered by some banks and insurance companies to people over 60, you will be offered only modest values until age 70 or 75 – for these schemes, the older you are, the better. So if you are thinking about equity release as the way of financing your pension, you should probably think of taking out an interest-only mortgage and repaying that from equity release after some years – assuming that you are planning to retire some while before age 70.

Buying and selling, letting and renting

It would take another book to detail how to buy and sell a house, but there are some financial guidelines that are important.

When you buy:
- ◆ Draw up a budget: the mortgage lenders' ratios are different from buy-to-let, and are typically three times the principal income plus one times the second, or two-and-a-half times the joint income.

- ◆ Work out an income and cash flow statement for the first year following your move: here, you need to include the costs relating to the house purchase – legal, removals, stamp duty.

- ◆ Estimate costs and timings of any work or improvements that you want; include any changes in how much you are likely to pay in council tax and the utilities – gas, electricity and telecoms.

When you sell:
- ◆ Decide on the minimum value you will accept.

- ◆ Contact several agents, preferably members of one of the professional bodies.

- ◆ Consider using more than one agent – this may cost more, but could increase your chances of a quick sale; do not necessarily choose the agent with the lowest fee.

When you let:
- ◆ Choose a letting agent who is registered with one of the professional associations.

- ◆ Make sure you have a solid contract, which will be the tenancy agreement.

- ◆ Form a view of the market in which you are operating and fix the rent accordingly.

When you rent:
- ◆ Contact a number of agents and explain exactly what you want.

- ◆ Go through the tenancy agreement – never sign something you do not understand.

- ◆ Be ready to provide references, some advance rent and a deposit.

These are the essentials of the three different equity release plans:

Roll-up mortgage

You take out an interest-only mortgage, but you do not pay any cash interest. The interest bill is rolled up and paid off, with the principal amount of the mortgage, when you and your spouse have died or gone into long-term care. The mortgage is likely to equal 25–30% of the value of your house. You can expect the choice of a lump sum or a drawdown scheme.

If you live a long time, the interest bill could become substantial (note: 7% a year doubles in 10 years) and the rates charged tend to be higher than on mortgages. Your children will not inherit the house unless they pay off the debt, though that will reduce the size of your estate for inheritance tax. You should get a guarantee of 'no negative equity' so that the mortgage and interest together will not represent a charge on your estate, however long you live. You remain the owner of your house.

Home reversion

Here you sell part of your house to the financial institution; you should get a rather higher proportion of its market value, probably around 40% (so that if you sell the institution half of your house, you will receive 20% of its market value). When you both die or go into long-term care, the house will be sold and the financial institution will take its share – including appreciation on its share of your house since the reversion plan was set up. Under home reversion, you cease to own your house; you have a lifetime tenancy.

As we are all living longer, you can see why roll-up mortgages and home reversion schemes favour the over 70s: the younger you are, the longer the bank or insurance company is out of its money.

The Financial Services Authority regulates life-time mortgages and is expected in the future to supervise home reversion.

Home income
You effectively turn your house (or part of it) into an annuity. You should do rather better this way than if you took cash and bought the annuity yourself. You have an interest-only mortgage, and part of your annuity income meets the interest payments. Home income plans are now less popular than lifetime mortgages or home reversion.

Is equity release for you?
Equity release schemes are likely to have greatest appeal to people whose house represents a large proportion of the assets they have built up to acquire a pension. For many people, their pension will have proved disappointingly low, while the equity in their house is their only substantial realisable asset. But remember: you will probably need to start with a straight mortgage because equity release only starts to be significant when you and your spouse are 70 or older. You also need to think carefully (and discuss it with your family and heirs) because these schemes can be difficult to unlock once you have committed yourself: an annuity, for instance, is fixed once you have signed up.

SHOULD YOU BUY A SECOND HOME?
So far, we have looked at the situation where you have your one home and you are exploiting its value to help you towards

affording a decent pension. But as you are working on the belief that property is a sound long-term investment, would it make sense to buy a second home?

Many people find a second home appealing, maybe as a country or seaside escape from urban pressure. If you believe property values will continue to rise, then a second home could also prove a good investment. But you also need to consider the tax implications. It would make good tax sense, when you retire, to sell your principal house (your main residence) and move into the former second home. The gain on your main residence will be free of tax; you simply need to notify the Inland Revenue of the change.

But what makes good tax sense may not fit in with your plans: you may want to sell your second home to pay for your pension and continue to live in your principal house – or you may want to sell both houses and live somewhere completely different, perhaps abroad.

Don't forget capital gains tax

You need to pause at this point, because if you sell your second home, you are looking at a bill for capital gains tax: only your principal residence is free from tax when you sell. If you can plan ahead, you could move into your second home and make that your principal residence before you sell; to be effective, all that should happen some years before. If you have to go ahead and sell your second home, it will help if it is in joint names (two allowances instead of one), you should be able to offset the cost of improvements, and you will get taper relief depending on how long you have owned your second home. But even after 10 years' ownership, you still face paying tax at your highest rate on 60% of your gain.

A holiday let?

There is another solution – to turn your second home into a holiday let, which counts as a business. The rules are somewhat complex, but the benefits are considerable.

Benefits

As a holiday let is a business, you pay much less capital gains tax when you sell: after two years, you pay tax on only 25% of the gain. For a higher rate taxpayer, this means you will pay just 10%. By the same logic, the income from a holiday let counts as business earnings, from which you can, for example, pay pension contributions. (By contrast, if you simply let the property, the rent would count as investment income.) In a holiday let, you can also get capital allowances on furniture and kitchen equipment – and if you lose money, you can offset this against your other income.

Rules

Now for the rules you have to follow to enjoy these advantages. You have to arrange to let on a commercial basis, with the property available for a minimum 140 days during the tax year and actually let for at least half that time, i.e. 70 days. You should not let to the same person for more than 31 days, which means (the rules get complex at this point) that you will let to at least three different people during each tax year.

So you want to be a landlord?

You may find that being a landlord is enjoyable and profitable. Being a landlord is now more popular than at any time since the 19th century, and letting is recognised as a way of benefiting from a second home – or a third or fourth. If your thoughts go beyond a second home, you are looking at the world of buy-to-let as your way to a satisfactory pension.

SUMMARY

◆ Realise the capital locked in your house:
- sell and move to a smaller house
- borrow on mortgage
- let-to-buy.

◆ Equity release especially for the over 70s:
- roll-up mortgage
- home reversion
- home income.

◆ Equity release plans generally mean your house is sold when you and your spouse die or go into long-term care – so think about the impact on your family and heirs.

◆ Buy a second home and sell your main house free of gains tax.

◆ If you sell your second home you are liable to capital gains tax.

◆ Consider a holiday let: there are strict rules, but attractive tax breaks.

BUY-TO-LET – AND OTHER OPTIONS

Buy-to-let – buying a house in order to let it out and profit from the rental income – was widespread in the 19th and early 20th century, but then disappeared until just a few years ago. And since its revival, buy-to-let has boomed:

◆ Property has proved a good investment: house prices have doubled over the past five years, while shares have stood still.

♦ Being a landlord has gained greater public acceptance.

♦ Lenders have been willing to provide a range of buy-to-let mortgages. The important change is that lenders have brought their interest rates into line with those charged to owner-occupiers and now take rental income into account.

The investment appeal

Unlike other investments, buy-to-let demands a range of individual skills and involvement (see *The Buy To Let Handbook* by Tony Booth, published by How To Books) even if you sub-contract the management to letting agents. But if you believe that property is going to help provide your pension in the years ahead, then you are likely to be involved in buy-to-let. The growth of buy-to-let is still recent: the Association of Retail Letting Agents have been logging the market for around ten years. From an investment perspective, the starting-point has to be the government's own research, which predicts that by 2021 tenant numbers will have increased by 46% to 3.5 million, so indicating a growing demand for rented property. Because house prices have been rising, first-time buyers have been stepping onto the property ladder at a later age, and so renting for longer.

There has been an increase in the number of single occupants (reflecting, for example, rising divorce rates) who may find it harder to buy. Almost 8 million people, it is estimated, are living alone. Student numbers have been increasing, and some middle-class families have their first taste of buy-to-let when they buy a house in a university town for their son or daughter.

The investment question

The principal investment issue on buy-to-let is risk. If buy-to-let is to provide your pension, and you have only one buy-to-let property, a great deal depends on your making the right choice. This is underlined by the wide regional differences: London was a natural starting-point for buy-to-let, but after a few years the market moved into over-supply, and more recently the north-east of England has proved a better investment. The answer has to be to spread your investment. According to industry figures, landlords on average now own between five and six properties – though a number own a single buy-to-let, often within 20 miles of their home.

You will probably start your equity investment in buy-to-let by re-mortgaging your own house. Over a period you could build up your equity to say £100,000; with mortgage levels at 75%, you would then have funds available which you could use to buy two or perhaps three properties – probably not in London or the south-east initially, but perhaps in a university town for student lets or near a hospital in the north of England.

What sort of yield?

Assessing the yields obtained by buy-to-let investors depends on industry surveys: a recent survey showed an average of just over 6% before tax and management fees. Returns were highest in the East Midlands and lowest in Greater London. These yields were probably helped by borrowing: if you arranged fixed-interest debt at reasonable rates when the overall market is rising, your equity will improve – as any company finance director will confirm.

Don't buy what you like

One of the fundamental lessons of buy-to-let is to avoid buying a property which you would like to live in. Buy-to-let is a business operation: you have to decide who is your target tenant and then evaluate the sort of property you should buy and its location.

You also need to look at the running costs of your buy-to-let operation. You must allow for legal and survey costs. If you are employed or self-employed, you will probably want to sub-contract to a letting agency, who will take 10–15% of the rental income for their trouble. Unless you are a happy DIYer, you will need to identify a builder who can sort out the landlord's repair and maintenance obligations.

Above all, you need to take a medium to long-term view, and be alert at all times to keeping down the cost of borrowing: over the past few years, re-mortgaging has become of particular importance to buy-to-let landlords.

Take a cool view

You need to take a cool view of what you buy: while you should not take a short-term view of your investment, if you feel that you have made a mistake then you should sell. Evidence suggests that two-thirds of buy-to-let investors aim to keep their properties for more than 10 years and as many as one in five for over 20 years. This fits with the number of younger investors in buy-to-let – more than a quarter aged between 25 and 35.

What often matters most in this decision is your level of borrowing. An initial 75% should give you reasonable leeway, and this level will fall as house values rise. A higher level of borrowing could cause problems (especially if you have to lower the rent when you face more than average voids – gaps between lets) and landlords' average borrowing is now between 50% and 60%.

Buy-to-let – an example

David Taylor earns a salary of £40,000 and has a £60,000 mortgage on his house. He wants to acquire a buy-to-let apartment for £160,000 and can get together £40,000 cash for a 25% deposit; he expects to receive rent of £10,000 a year – a yield of just over 6%.

He wants a £120,000 mortgage. Here is how the lender will look at his application:

♦ David's earned income is £40,000, which the lender values at a 3.25 multiple, which equals £130,000.

♦ David's forecast of £10,000 rental income is accepted (he gets confirmation from a letting agent) which the lender values at a 6.5 multiple, which equals £65,000.

♦ His borrowing capacity is therefore rated at £195,000; the lender offsets David's existing mortgage of £60,000, which leaves him with available capacity of £135,000.

David therefore gets his mortgage request for £120,000 and is free to go and acquire his buy-to-let property.

How to get your money

If recent years' trends continue, house values and rentals will continue to rise, though maybe at a rather slower rate. Fundamental to your plan is that you are operating in a taxable area: your rental is in principle taxable, as is the gain on your properties when you come to sell.

If you are employed or self-employed and building your pension pot, you need to reckon in the tax effects. (The large numbers who own a single buy-to-let have the option of selling their main home free of gains tax and then moving into the buy-to-let, which then becomes their principal residence; in that case it would make more sense to buy what you like.)

Keeping capital gains tax down

Though your rental income is taxable, you can offset interest costs, letting agents' fees and maintenance charges. Your capital gain is charged in the usual way (remember: a doubled allowance if the buy-to-let is jointly owned with your partner) and you will be able to offset the cost of improvements, together with agents', legal and advertising costs on the sale. When you come to sell, it makes sense to arrange one sale per tax year to gain most benefit from your allowance.

There are other, sophisticated, ways to cut your tax bill: if you treat the buy-to-let property as your main residence, even for one year, your tax bill can be significantly reduced. There are further concessions when you sell your former main residence which has been let either entirely or in part.

Two major supports

There are two major supports for buy-to-let. On the demand side, the official figures reflect the national trend towards a higher number of smaller households, a growing student population and more people waiting and saving for their first house purchase. On the supply side, there is always the risk that a number of landlords will decide to pull out and put buy-to-let properties onto an unwilling market. In property, this tends to happen when owners are over-borrowed – but as overall loans to value are in the 50–60% range for buy-to-let landlords, this seems unlikely to become a problem.

All this assumes no sudden rise in interest rates and no sudden check in income growth!

OTHER PROPERTY OPTIONS

Most people who see property as the way to provide their pensions will think of buying a second home or moving into buy-to-let. But there are other ways to access the property market.

Buying shares in property companies

One option is to buy shares in property companies, which are normally divided between property investment companies and development companies. Property investment companies typically hold a mature portfolio, as a rule mainly commercial with some industrial property. Property companies tend to avoid residential investment. You need to look at the spread and type of the investments.

In property development companies you are largely backing the skills of the board and the chief executive. You will need to look at the record and assess the development plans that will be set out in the report and accounts. One test is to compare the shares' asset values with their price in the stock market: this will show you what sort of premium you are paying for the skills of the directors. Over the next year or so, choice will be widened by the long-awaited creation of Real Estate Investment Trusts (REITs) which will offer a wide spread of managed property in a tax-efficient structure.

Property unit and investment trusts, and bonds

There are a number of property unit and investment trusts, some quite large. You can often get a reasonable dividend yield, and there is the attraction that they can invest in commercial property, which is another way to spread your risk.

Property shares and unit and investment trusts are essentially stock market investments, and they also suffered during the dark market days of 2000–3. For this reason, many people consider property shares and trusts as a specialist form of stock exchange investment, as opposed to direct involvement in property

A fund for house prices

Even as a passive investor, you can profit from the rise in house prices. This is through a property bond, issued by a building society. You open, say, a five-year account and at the end of that time you are paid interest equal to 85% of the average rise in the Halifax House Price Index (Halifax and Nationwide both publish authoritative house price data). Your capital is guaranteed.

If you believe that house prices will go on rising, this investment has appeal, but be aware:

◆ You have to tie up your capital for five years.

◆ If house prices do rise over the five years, your gain will come as income rather than capital, so it would make sense to use a cash mini ISA to make the interest tax-free.

◆ If house prices go into reverse, as they did in the early 1990s, you get your money back. Your loss would then be the opportunity cost on your capital, i.e. what you could otherwise have done with the money: if you put it into a cash mini ISA, you would be 25% better off at the end of five years.

SUMMARY

◆ Buy-to-let has become popular in the past few years because overall – not so much last year – house prices out-performed shares by a wide margin. Being a landlord is now more acceptable, and finance has become widely available.

◆ New social trends are helping – a growing number of smaller households, first-time buyers waiting longer to get on the property ladder, students and divorced men and women.

◆ Risk is an issue if you own only one or just a few buy-to-let properties (the typical landlord owns five or six properties).

◆ Treat buy-to-let as a business and do not buy what you would like – unless you plan later to sell your main residence and move into the buy-to-let.

◆ Be prepared to take a long-term view of your buy-to-let property: budget your likely income and capital gains when you come to sell.

The Seventh Step – Use Insurance

Until just a few years ago, insurance was the great pillar on which to build your pension assets: with-profits bonds became the major savings medium, several times larger than all National Savings put together. Then came the stock market setback of 2000–3, the sad tale of Equitable Life, and insurance companies imposing significant penalties in people who wanted to cash in their policies. Mutterings about opaqueness and high charges turned into loud and damaging criticism.

However, there are two insurance products worth considering: one is still a with-profits policy, but only for people who are prepared to lock their money away for at least five years and who positively do not want to buy their own investments. The second, which offers possibilities if you do your homework, is a traded or 'second-hand' endowment policy.

WITH-PROFITS BONDS

There are two schools of thought on with-profits policies: the optimists say that the worst is over, companies are re-basing their prices so that a new buyer does not have to pay for past problems and the advantages remain – smoothed growth without all the ups and downs of the stock market.

The doubters' case is that the 2000–3 slide inflicted serious long-term damage – witness the companies which have pulled out of the with-profits market and the number of changes within the industry.

The investment basics

The simple theory of a with-profits policy is that you invest, say, £20,000 looking at a 25-year term. You check the company's financial strength, so you will probably end up with one of the half dozen household names. You consider how they allocate their assets between equities and fixed-interest and you look over past performance. As ever, you buy through a discount broker who should save you between £500 and £1,000. If you are a higher-rate taxpayer, you have at present the ability to withdraw up to 5% a year for 20 years, with the tax deferred. Even if you go over the limit, payments are made net of basic rate tax at 22%, so that you are charged only an extra 18%, not the full 40%. (With-profits policies are not suitable for non-taxpayers or low-rate payers as the tax deducted cannot be reclaimed.)

How top-slicing works

Even if you, as a higher-rate taxpayer, have a substantial gain when your policy matures, the Inland Revenue will allow for the number of years you have held the bond. This is done through 'top-slicing', where your gain is divided by the number of years: you pay tax only on the proportion that results.

As a standard rate taxpayer, you will have no extra tax to pay – but take care if the gain pushes you into the higher tax bracket. This underlines the case for the bond to be held jointly with your lower tax-paying spouse, or held entirely by them.

Today's picture

Looking at today's reality, you will find that equity proportions in insurers' asset portfolios have shrunk, mainly in response to the dire performance in 2000–3: many of the leading names have less than 50% in ordinary shares, some less than 40%. This defensive switch is likely to limit performance in future years.

Policy bonuses have been reduced, typically to around 4% – which has an immediate impact if you want to take the annual 5% free of immediate tax. If you withdraw more than the bonus rate – 5% against 4% – then you need to recognise that you are eating into capital, even if the insurance company allows you to draw that much.

So you look at actual performance over recent years, and you find annual compound returns of between 4% and 5%. Not great, you think, but not bad – and ahead of inflation. But there is a big hidden snag: these are fund values and not, repeat not, the values you can get your hands on.

What you can get – or can't

Two things reduce the amount of money you can put in your pocket. One is the built-in penalty for early surrender: if your circumstances change, and you need your money within the first five years, you will be charged a penalty which could amount to 5–10% of your total policy.

But the big difference comes from MVA – the market value adjuster, really the market value reducer. Essentially, this means that if you want to cash in say, at a time when markets are faltering, you will be charged a penalty, which has been of the order of 20% which some companies are starting to reduce. The companies say that MVA protects people who stay in a fund as opposed to those who want out in difficult times. But the fact remains, if you need to access your money – or if you want to change your insurer – you stand to be hit.

Costs and tax

What do the insurance companies charge you? The answer does not come in simple form, but is expressed as a reduction in yield. You put in your £20,000, a 6% growth rate is assumed (that is an official figure) and you are told how much the yield will be reduced, looking at a projected 10-year value. So you compare the reduction in yield with the official growth assumption and get an indication of total charges. For the major insurance companies, the answer over the 10 years seem to lie between 15% and 20%.

Higher-rate taxpayers are attracted by the ability to withdraw 5% a year free of immediate tax – with the tax deferred for 20 years or until you cash in. (In current conditions the industry view is that 4% a year is the maximum you can take without eating into capital). If that ability continues, it would represent a big plus for with-profit bonds; but recently the Treasury has been dropping heavy hints that this concession was being looked over. Maybe the Treasury will decide to forget its review; maybe, if it does stop the concession, policies already in existence will escape. But there has to be some uncertainty.

WITH-PROFITS BONDS – TO SUM UP

With-profits bonds could prove helpful in reaching your target for pension assets, provided:

- you are prepared if necessary to stay the full length of time for your investment

- you understand that if you do cash in, especially during the early years, you could face a significant penalty

- you have sufficient other investments that you can realise for cash at short notice if the need arises

- if you are a higher-rate taxpayer, and aiming to exploit the annual 5% cash-in facility, then you appreciate that this may not last

- you can accept that the insurance companies' charges are reasonable in return for the smoothed investment performance which with-profits bonds offer.

DISTRIBUTION BONDS

Many people remain attracted by the bond wrapper, especially the ability, unless the law changes, to cash in 5% each year of their original investment free of immediate tax. (Because this is not regarded as income, drawing 5% each year will not affect your other allowances.)

Distribution bonds are an income-oriented variant of with-profits bonds which over recent years have out-performed high street instant access accounts. Distribution bonds' portfolios show a similar mix to those with-profits bonds, with some bias towards fixed-interest investments.

The major difference with with-profits bonds is that there is no 'smoothing' effect, that makes distribution bonds easier to analyse: performance is reflected in the payments and therefore in the price. Several of the major insurance companies sell distribution bonds, and you can have income paid monthly.

Charges tend to be in line with those of corporate bond unit trust funds, though some companies extract a penalty for surrender during the first five years. If you want a low-risk income from money that you do not need for several years, then distribution bonds are worth considering.

BUYING A SECOND-HAND INSURANCE POLICY

The concept is simple: one used endowment policy, careful owner, needs several years' premiums to realise. For the investor who chooses with care, a traded endowment policy can help towards building your pension assets – with some useful side-benefits on timing and tax.

The traded endowment policy (TEP) market took off when people began to realise, with falling stock markets, that their endowment policies were not going to pay off their mortgages, as they had expected. Millions of households were affected – according to one estimate, around one quarter of all families in the UK.

Faced with this problem of how to clear their mortgage, many people decided to surrender their policy back to the insurer – to discover that they could get more by selling in the marketplace. Now the Financial Services Authority requires insurers to tell policyholders that they can sell in the market, so people are encouraged to get quotes from brokers. (The market covers with-profits endowment policies, as opposed to unit-linked.)

Buying a TEP is not complex: you decide how much you want to spend in order to buy the policy and allow for the premiums you will have to pay until the policy matures. You have to decide on the maturity date – which can be useful if you have a particular obligation to meet in the years ahead, such as school fees – and select the insurance company. As a buyer, you will realise that the number of people trying to sell endowments should give you a reasonable choice.

As buying second-hand TEPs has become more popular, some insurance companies will allow you to pay off all the remaining premiums by means of a single contribution.

How to buy
The first, and most important, step in buying a TEP is to relate your price to the guaranteed element in the policy – which is the amount assured plus bonuses which have already been allocated. If your price comes under this level, your capital is protected: you will only be exposed by the ratio of future premiums to future bonuses, which in any case should be small in relation to your initial capital.

Bonuses in the time to come will probably be less than in recent years – they are likely to stay close to actual investment returns – but if you buy, say, a 25-year policy with 10 years to go, you will have some useful bonuses already locked in. Something of a question overhangs the terminal bonus, which is paid when the policy matures; this is inevitably affected by stock market conditions at the time.

The second, also important, step in buying a TEP is to choose one of the major insurers, whose investment performance has generally proved reasonable. Having a policy with one of the major names will also help if you need to re-sell the TEP before it finally matures. (If you find that you need to sell, your only constraint is the market: there are none of the penalties which affect holders of with-profits bonds.)

Tax issues

TEP policies come in two sorts: qualifying and non-qualifying, as defined by the Inland Revenue. Their rules are complex, but most types of policies that involve you in paying regular premiums are qualifying. What matters is that you get clear guidance from the broker on the policy category before you commit, because the tax treatment is different. In a qualifying policy, the gain is classed as capital, whereas the gain on a non-qualifying policy is classed as income and your tax bill is calculated on the assumption that basic rate tax has been paid.

TEPs therefore offer a useful advantage in tax planning. Taking profits from qualifying TEPs will enable you, at a low level of risk, to make use of your annual allowance for capital gains tax. This means that you and your spouse can realise profits of £17,000 a year, and rising, tax-free. That is a useful way to build your pension assets.

Even if the policy is non-qualifying, a higher rate taxpayer will gain from top-slicing – as with a with-profit bond – while your tax rate will be 18% rather than the full 40%.

Judging performance

Calculating the performance of TEPs is not, unfortunately, that simple. You receive your cash sum from the insurance company, representing the policy proceeds – the sum assured, all the declared bonuses and usually a terminal bonus. To get that money, you had to pay over the initial capital to buy the policy and continue the premiums until the policy matured. The difference between what you receive and what you paid out, annualised over the number of years, gives you an annual compound rate of return. Happily, TEPs have become a reasonably sophisticated market – some estimates put the turnover at £10 million a week – so that your broker will be able to guide you on yields. For a lay person, a good basic test remains that the amount you pay to buy the policy is less than the sum assured plus the bonuses already declared.

A series of TEPs?

You and your spouse could take out a series of TEPs, maturing over a succession of years, with the gains coming as tax-free from qualifying policies so long as they fall within the annual gains tax limit. This should not be difficult to achieve, for TEPs are not especially expensive, with most costing up to £30,000 and a number between £5,000 and £12,000.

If the policy is non-qualifying, then it would make sense for you to hold it jointly with your spouse – even better for a low- or non-taxpayer to hold the policy. A basic-rate taxpayer should have no further liability.

A TEP trust?

You may like the idea of buying a TEP, but do not want the hassle of paying regular premiums or be concerned that you may choose the wrong policy. In this case, you can buy shares in one of the quoted endowment investment trusts.

Applying the investment trust idea to TEPs means that the trust will hold, say, 1,500 to 2,000 policies with a pre-arranged winding-up date. There is no dividend, but investors' return comes from the growth of capital: one trust, wound up after an 11-year life, gave shareholders an effective annual return of around 7.5% – at a low level of risk.

SUMMARY

◆ Buy a traded endowment policy (TEP) issued by one of the leading insurers.

◆ Try to make sure that your initial capital is covered by the amount assured plus bonuses that have already been declared.

◆ Link the maturity dates with any of your known future obligations, e.g. paying school fees.

◆ Consider buying several smaller TEPs, to give you a series of receipts – plus the ability to use your yearly capital gains tax allowance, if the policies are qualifying.

◆ If the policies are non-qualifying, gains will be taxed as income – so the policies should be owned by a low- or non-taxpayer.

◆ If buying a policy and keeping up the premiums seems too much hassle, think about an endowment investment trust.

$$\left(\begin{array}{c}8\end{array}\right)$$

If Things Go Wrong

This book shows you how to build up resources in order to pay for a comfortable pension, so that you can retire, cash in – and you and your spouse or partner can then look forward to perhaps 20 years of happy retirement. That picture will apply to many people, perhaps most, but not to everyone. Things can go wrong: you may become separated or divorced, you or your spouse may fall ill, your financial decisions may not work out, you may die.

IF YOU GET DIVORCED

Divorce and tax

Income tax is not a major element in divorce: the married couple's allowance is only available to people over 70 (born before 6 April 1935) and then offers a mere 10% reduction. The allowance is given in full in the year of separation or death of either spouse.

But your capital gains tax liability may be affected. There is a gains tax concession for three years on the transfer of the family home and the bill is softened even after three years.

If a second home (i.e. not the family home) or any other property is transferred, then there is an exemption from stamp duty – nowadays a worthwhile saving.

Transferring shares

Many divorce settlements involve the transfer of shares – here, timing is important. There is no capital gains tax payable when assets are transferred between a husband and wife, and this continues to apply in a tax year when a married couple are living together. After that, tax has to be paid.

The moral is clear: when a settlement involves the transfer of shares, or valuable furniture or paintings, all this should be done in that final tax year.

If inheritance tax is a concern, the situation is rather easier: the normal exemption between spouses continues after separation until divorce – and even then there is a concession to transfers which are made to a former spouse for their maintenance and that of any children.

Pensions now in the frame

The biggest change of all to the finances of divorce came only a few years ago, when pension rights were included in a settlement. Before that, a divorcee had no access to their former spouse's potentially large pension assets. Under a recent ruling, pension assets do not form part of a capital settlement; the pension income is shared out.

All pensions are included; the scheme works simply on the basis that the spouse with a pension faces a pension debit while the other is given a pension credit. The pension credit can stay in the existing scheme – so that a divorced wife could draw a pension from the same scheme that is paying her former husband. Alternatively, the pension credit can be used in another scheme: the choice will often depend on the attractions of the original pension plan, because a transfer is likely to involve some costs.

(Only the basic state pension cannot be shared.)

Under the new pension rules, where a divorcing couple share a pension, each share will count towards each one's £1.5 million (2006–7) lifetime limit.

IF YOU FALL ILL

Many senior executives like to joke that they are worth more dead than alive: their widow or widower would receive four times their salary together with a pension equal to two-thirds of what they would have been paid. What bothers such people is the risk of injury or illness.

Your first step should be to work out your liabilities, which will probably be the mortgage and perhaps future school fees. If you fall ill, you need to reflect on what help would be available: your employer might keep you on the payroll for six months, which would at least buy some time.

If you think you would still have a deficit, then you need to think about insurance:

◆ **Life assurance** – rates have become competitive, so you could buy over the Internet or go to a broker.

◆ **Income protection** – a long-term policy which will protect your income if you are unable to work through illness or injury.

◆ **Mortgage protection** – often linked with income protection, and has the advantage that the term decreases as the mortgage is gradually repaid.

♦ **Critical illness** – designed to pay a cash sum, free of tax, when you are diagnosed as suffering from a predetermined serious condition such as cancer or a stroke.

♦ **Health insurance** – offered by some employers; if you buy it yourself, premiums can be expensive, but health insurance resembles car insurance: if you are willing to meet a generous first portion of any claim, then the premiums will be reduced.

Many companies will combine several different types of plan into one package. Which you choose has to depend on your own judgment, given your medical history and that of your immediate family.

WHAT HAPPENS WHEN YOU DIE?

More than half of people in the UK have not made a will. Do not, repeat not, join them. If you want to direct where your assets go on your death, if you are living with a partner (other than same-sex) unmarried and if you want to save inheritance tax, then you need to make a will. If you don't make a will, the intestacy rules will apply. If you have children, your spouse will receive any jointly owned property, but will then inherit only the first £125,000 of the remaining estate. Everything else will be divided into two. Your spouse could change this, but if the children are under 18, the court would have to agree; you do not want to leave that situation behind.

Your unmarried heterosexual partner, as the law stands at present, has virtually no legal rights to your estate (unless they were dependent). A will is therefore essential to direct where your property goes; such a partner, unlike a spouse, has no inheritance tax exemption.

Avoiding inheritance tax (IHT)

If you want to avoid inheritance tax (who doesn't?) then you should make a will. As a first step, work out how much will be paid. No IHT will be due if you leave everything to your spouse, but his or her estate will suffer correspondingly greater tax on the second death.

Working out IHT liability is simple: you value all of your assets, deduct the annual tax-free allowance – known as the nil rate band – which amounts to £285,000 for 2006–7 and calculate 40% on all the rest. That is the IHT.

Accountants and lawyers have devised many ingenious ways to avoid inheritance tax, but there is one simple and effective route. You and your spouse make similar wills, so that on the first death an amount equal to the nil rate band goes to the children and everything else to the surviving spouse. No IHT will be due, and the family has saved inheritance tax of £114,000 (40% of £285,000) on the second death. To make a will, go to a solicitor.

Cutting inheritance tax – an example

John Lillee wants to give away as much as possible out of income by means of exempt gifts – he would find it difficult to hand over a sizeable lump sum and he is concerned he would have to live for seven years after making the gift if inheritance tax is to be avoided.

So he gives away £750 a year to each of his four children, which makes use of the £3,000 a year annual exemption. In addition he makes gifts of £250 each year to friends and more distant relations – taking care that the two groups of gifts do not overlap!

John agrees with his accountant that he can also give away £2,000 a year out of income without affecting his standard of living or drawing on capital. He understands that this £2,000 a year should be placed on a regular basis, so he decides to pay premiums on insurance policies. These policies, which are on his own life, were written in trust for each of the children just before Budget Day 2006. This means that when he dies the money from the policies will be paid direct to the four and will not form part of his estate for tax purposes. John has arranged a series of exempt gifts which will be wholly free from inheritance tax when he dies.

Term assurance

One widely used solution is to buy term assurance, where the insurers will pay out a fixed sum if the policyholder dies within the predetermined time. Premiums will depend on the amount of cover you want and also on your lifestyle – you will pay more if you smoke or if you take part in hazardous sports. You need to allow for any payment that will come from your employer's pension scheme.

You can buy term assurance through a broker or online. Many of the deals will be execution-only, which means that you will have to decide how much you need. As ever, it will pay to shop around.

New IHT rules – an example

Never forget: any gift made after 17 March 1986 could be affected by the new treatment of pre-owned assets.

John Johnston gave his son, Ray, a portfolio of shares which had been recommended by his broker. That was in April 1986, when the shares were worth £30,000.

Twenty years later, the shares have risen to £250,000 and Ray decides to cash in.

John falls ill and finds that his pension is smaller than he had expected. So Ray decides to use part of the funds from the share sale to buy his father a small flat.

They are both horrified to learn that John will now become liable for income tax through a charge on a pre-owned asset. Their adviser points out that, under the new rules, income tax is charged on an individual who has made a gift of an asset but still retains some benefit in it.

Their adviser also explains how unfair this rule is. If John had given Ray £30,000 in cash and Ray had bought the same shares, the charge would have been avoided because the gift of cash was made more than seven years before the flat was occupied.

POWER OF ATTORNEY

Senior executives' other nightmare is that they are lying injured in hospital, unable to handle their financial affairs – maybe even unable to access their bank account. Banks and insurance companies will try to help your spouse or relatives, but there are formal restrictions on what they can do. So you need a power of attorney.

You will probably have given your solicitor a power of attorney to complete the sale or purchase of a house. You gave this power for a specific purpose, perhaps with a particular time reference. What you need now to give your spouse – and probably exchange with each other – is a general power of attorney. A solicitor will draw this up, and it can be shown to the bank or other organisations as necessary, say to access a deposit account.

Enduring Power of Attorney

Even this may not prove entirely effective, because a power of attorney will lapse if the person giving the power can no longer give instructions. So if you are laid up in hospital, unconscious after a car crash, your power of attorney will no longer operate.

The answer to this conundrum (also worth considering as you and your partner get older, or if one of you does a lot of air travel) is an enduring power of attorney. The sensible course is to exchange with your partner and to include your solicitor. If you want to play really safe, you should not name a partner in the law firm (in case they die first) but either use the firm's trust corporation or a formula such as 'John Smith, or failing him a partner nominated by the senior partner at the time'. This operation is not expensive, and your family will be most grateful (and save time and trouble) if you are unlucky and crash your car.

HOW TO GET ADVICE

You might feel that you need advice. Maybe you are busy, travelling a great deal, maybe you feel out of your depth in building up assets so that you can afford a decent pension. You need to answer two questions before you contact an adviser:

◆ Why are you looking for advice?
◆ What objectives you are trying to achieve?

You also need to be clear as to how much money you have available, and for how long.

Choosing a broker

Many people will look for advice in choosing shares or unit trusts, which points you towards an investment manager or a stockbroker. The trade association will provide a list of firms, but you will have to decide which one to follow. A personal recommendation is best, from either a friend, colleague, solicitor or your accountant. Otherwise, you will have to rely on your own judgment – go and see three or four brokers and decide which you find most effective. Over the long run, this will be time well spent.

Brokers operate in three different ways:

◆ **Execution-only**. These offer no advice or management (that may be available separately) but they are much the cheapest if you are happy to take your own decisions. They will operate by telephone, but most effectively over the Internet. They will also trade shares within PEPs and ISAs. Your shares will be held in a nominee or similar account. Some execution-only brokers offer research and data assistance.

◆ **Advisory**. The broker makes suggestions, and you have to decide whether or not to accept. The problem here is often a practical one: you may lose out unless you are in a position to give the broker an early response – and the adviser themselves may get discouraged.

◆ **Discretionary**. This is a popular way of working, which many advisers prefer. You work out guidelines with the broker and tell them any of your likes or dislikes. (This is best agreed in writing.) The broker then buys and sells shares without having to ask for your prior agreement – though you get a contract note after each transaction so that you know what deals are taking place. Advisers prefer discretionary agreements because they are able to act quickly. For many people, the choice lies between execution-only where you decide and a discretionary agreement, where the broker decides within an agreed strategy.

Whatever the type of service, you will get details of all deals after a few days and the advisory or discretionary broker will send you valuations, at least twice a year. You need to spend some time over the valuations, which give you the data on how your portfolio is performing.

Paying a broker

You pay a broker a pre-agreed commission rate whenever you buy and sell shares. (When you buy, you will also have to pay stamp duty and a levy to the City Takeover Panel if the deal amounts to over £10,000.) The cheapest deals are online, and to keep costs down you need to use a PC if you want to handle your own investments. The more expensive trades will be when you use the telephone and hold your own certificates.

You will pay a separate fee if you want investment management and there may be charges if you ask for administrative services, such as using the broker's nominee account.

One common fallacy: it is not true that you have to be extremely wealthy to use a broker. Some brokers will welcome portfolios of £25,000: a useful starting-point will be the broking firm which works for – and is probably owned by – your bank.

General financial advice

You may need more help than just in buying and selling shares – perhaps with areas such as pensions, mortgages, insurance and cash management. About 30,000 firms give advice in these sectors: the former distinction, between tied and independent advisers, is being changed. Tied advisers offer advice only on the products of a particular company or group of companies – they are often employees.

An independent financial adviser (IFA) can cover the entire marketplace to find what you want: the essential case for going to an IFA is that they can arrange to meet your objectives more cheaply and effectively than you could by yourself – even if you access the Internet. There is now also a multi-tied adviser, a combination of the two.

Mortgage advice

For many people, making the right mortgage decision will be one of the most important they make and they will look for advice. Mortgage advisers have been organised differently from financial and investment advisers – it is only in the last few years that they have had to register with the Financial Services Authority.

The choice of mortgages has become unusually wide. Discounted mortgages offer a reduced rate for a term. Mortgages can be fixed, deferred, variable and now 'capped and collared' (predetermined maximum and minimum levels).

To address this complex area, mortgage advisers fall into one of three groups:

♦ advisers who sell the products of one lender
♦ advisers who offer the products of several lenders
♦ advisers who cover the entire market to meet your demands.

Finding an IFA

You can get a list of independent financial advisers from the trade association, and you need to decide how you will judge. Are you looking for a particular speciality, say pensions, or do you want an IFA who is near where you live or work? Do you prefer a male or female adviser? When you meet your adviser, the FSA has three principal suggestions:

◆ Don't be embarrassed to ask questions.
◆ Don't go ahead unless you are completely happy.
◆ Never sign a blank form, leaving the adviser to complete later.

Paying an IFA

Going to an IFA will cost, in fees and/or commission. On fees, most IFAs charge between £80 and £200 an hour, according to the industry – though you may have to add on 17.5% VAT. On commission, which is how most financial products are sold, the IFA will keep what is built into the product; they must tell you in advance how much they will get.

At one time, there was a move to end commission sales, on the grounds that advisers might put forward financial products that gave them the highest commission rather than the most suitable for their client. But at present, the fee and commission systems exist side by side. If you pay a fee, any commission that is built into the product would normally be invested back. Some IFAs offer a mix-and-match arrangement, charging a lower fee if they keep some commission. You have to ask.

HOW TO COMPLAIN

If you asked people what went wrong, probably the most common reply would be that their investments did not grow as fast as they had hoped. The final value failed to meet their target, so they feel entitled to complain. Alas, disappointment alone does not give you a basis to complain.

Essentially, you are entitled to complain when a financial product turns out badly because the firm concerned did something wrong. They may have overcharged you, given you bad advice or cost you money because of poor service. So what do you do?

Go to the firm

Your first step has to be to go to the firm, set out your complaint and show how much you have lost. It is important to get everything down on paper, so keep copies and make a note of any telephone conversations – if you want to be especially careful, send a letter to the firm confirming what was said.

Some complaints are resolved at this stage, when the firm offers you compensation. But you may feel that the firm is not treating you fairly – or they may not reply at all.

The next step: a choice

One possible next step is to go to the firm's trade association. Trade associations vary a good deal in terms of scope, relations with their members and above all in speed of response.

Or you may decide to approach the Financial Ombudsman Service, who deal with complaints about a wide range of services, including banking, insurance, personal pension plans, shares and unit trusts. And their service is free. At the time of writing, they could not help about most insurance and mortgage brokers and some types of equity release schemes; if these represent your problem, you will probably have to go to court.

Going to the Ombudsman

To approach the Ombudsman you need to meet one of two tests:

♦ The firm has sent you its final response but you are still unhappy, or

♦ Eight weeks have passed since you raised your complaint, but the firm still has not sent you its final response – or not replied at all.

You now need to fill in the Ombudsman's complaint form. Include all details and references, along with copies of your letters to the firm and their replies. You may decide to employ a solicitor or an IFA to help; if you do, be aware that you will almost certainly have to pay their costs yourself, even if the Ombudsman finds in your favour.

How the system works

The Ombudsman's first step will be to mediate: to try to get the firm to improve their offer and for you to accept. If mediation does not succeed, an adjudicator will go through your case and write to you to set out how your complaint should be resolved.

Your case may involve a formal decision by an Ombudsman. In that case, the firm have to accept – but you do not. You are free to go to court instead.

Small businesses can apply

Most of the Ombudsman's work comes from individuals' problems, but they will also deal with complaints from small businesses whose annual turnover is under £1 million. The objective is to keep the issues informal, so that you should not need the help of a solicitor or any special expertise. Anyone can complain on your behalf, but the Ombudsman will want to see written authority.

One major difference from court procedure is that decisions are taken on the basis of paperwork – in general without the need for face-to-face meetings. And the Ombudsman Service will not usually handle a case which has been considered by a court or where court proceedings are pending.

Don't miss the deadline

There is one important deadline: you need to send your completed complaint form within six months of the date on the firm's final response letter. Other time limits can apply – so don't leave it too long to complain once you know that there is a problem.

SUMMARY

◆ In a divorce, pensions are now included. There are concessions on transferring the family home – but gains on other assets will be tax-free only in the last year you and your spouse live together.

◆ Insurance is important – on your life, to protect your income, to cover your mortgage, to help you cope with critical illness and to provide private health insurance.

◆ Make a will: you and your spouse should each make one – essential if you want to cut back on the family's inheritance tax bill.

◆ Arrange a power of attorney – an enduring power of attorney to be completely secure (you need a solicitor both to make a will and to draw up a power of attorney).

◆ Consider whether you will need formal advice – establish what you want to achieve and how much you are prepared to pay.

◆ It is essential to keep records of your significant-sized financial transactions, just in case the firm involved does something wrong and for you and your family.

9

Be Sure to Win the Last Round

As any footballer or boxer will confirm, you can have a wonderful match but lose it in the last round. You can build up a handsome portfolio to beat the pension crisis but lose at least some of your advantage when it comes to buying your pension.

You need to start planning five years before you want to retire, because you will be taking decisions about a relatively large amount of money and these decisions will affect the rest of your post-retirement life.

'LIFESTYLE' CHANGE

Assume you have decided to retire at age 60, in five years' time. All that is certain (as the law stands now) is that you can buy an annuity from age 50 (to be raised to 55 by 2010) and that you MUST buy an annuity by age 75 – unless you are attracted by the new Alternatively Secured Pension. You could, in principle, leave the decision until you are 75 and live off the interest and dividends in the interim. That would be a high-risk strategy: your birthday could coincide with a stock market downturn or a slump in property prices.

As you are age 55, you could buy an annuity now, but the risks mirror those of waiting until the latest possible time, age 75, and your annuity will be much smaller. The most sensible course is to switch your investments wholly into fixed interest gradually over the five years before you retire, and then buy your annuity (if you follow the Wall Street formula, you will in any case be already half invested in fixed interest); alternatively, you can spread the buying of your annuity.

This is the 'lifestyle' change which some insurance companies operate; how far you follow it must be affected by your medical outlook, any other income you have and your own views of financial prospects over the years to come.

WHICH TYPE OF ANNUITY?

There are three types of annuity from which to choose – or mix, as no one compels you to put all your eggs in one basket:

- **Level**: your money income is fixed – this type will give you the highest immediate payment, but your real income will decline over the years as a result of inflation.

- **Escalator**: you give up some current income in return for a pre-agreed rate of increase in your annuity, generally between 2% and 5% a year.

- **Index-linked**: this will guarantee that your income will be maintained in real terms – now that inflation has fallen to around 2.5–3%, an annuity linked to retail prices is effectively a specific type of escalator annuity. (If retail prices were to fall, so would your annuity.)

Once you have made this major decision, you will have further choices, notably:

(i) Are you buying an annuity on your own single life, or do you also want an annuity for your spouse or partner when you die

– at the expense of current income?

(ii) Do you want a guarantee that your annuity will be paid for a minimum of 5 or 10 years?

(iii) Do you want to be paid monthly, quarterly or even yearly?

Remember: under the government's new 'simplification' rules, you can leave pension capital if you die before the age of 75 – but your heirs will have to pay tax at 35%. As it stands, this could cause hardship to many families over the years to come. If you die after age 75 you may not leave pension capital; your heirs have to take an annuity. If someone over 75 opts for an Alternatively Secured Pension, any assets remaining at death will be subject to IHT – unless the assets are used to benefit a spouse or partner.

There is no right or wrong in this area – except by hindsight. You have to make your own best judgment, possibly helped by professional advice.

[Note: This discussion centres on pension annuities or compulsory purchase annuities, which you have to buy before you reach 75. You should also be aware of ordinary or purchase life annuities, where you put investment money into an annuity. Ordinary annuities carry tax breaks, but are best suited for people who do not have dependants, or where they have been provided for.]

HELP FOR SMOKERS

One specialised area in the annuity market is 'impaired annuities' – higher payments made to people who are considered to face a shorter than average life expectancy. This includes anyone with a history of serious health problems, those engaged in heavy manual work and smokers.

Someone who has smoked for a number of years and still smokes 10 or more cigarettes a day will get annuity terms significantly better than for a non-smoker. Talk to your doctor if he knows the insurance world – he will be involved anyway if you want to pursue this idea.

CHOICE IN ANNUITIES

You don't have to decide to buy an annuity until age 75, and there is no requirement to put all your fund into an annuity if you retire before then. Here are some alternatives.

Phased retirement

This is applying the lifestyle plan to annuity buying. You decide to spread your purchases over, say, five years, in effect dividing your fund into five separate portfolios. You can easily spread them over more or less than five years and you don't necessarily have to make equal investments each year.

Income drawdown

You take the 25% cash from your fund – or a smaller proportion if you prefer – and the rest is invested. You can draw an income, within a range fixed by law, and at 75 you buy your annuity. You take an investment risk on your portfolio; for this reason the general view is that income drawdown is suitable for larger holdings of pension assets.

Open annuity

This is a recent development, aiming to ensure that funds which remain surplus after paying your pension can go to your heirs. With a classic annuity, all the fund stays with the insurance company when you die, unless you arranged a guarantee and/or a joint annuity. Assets can go to your heirs under income drawdown, but after tax. Arranging an open annuity is complex and suitable for substantial pension funds.

The government has recently introduced 'Alternatively Secured Pensions' to provide income from your fund beyond age 75, but the general reaction has been that you would probably be better off with a conventional annuity.

SPREAD YOUR RISK

You should approach pension buying in the same way you took your investment decisions. You do not put all your eggs in one basket and you diversify in order to reduce risk and to improve your growth possibilities. Assume that you put half your pension assets into a traditional type annuity; that is equivalent to putting half into fixed interest stocks. You have three options to complement your fixed-interest commitment.

- **With-profits annuities**: your annuity will perform in line with the insurance company's with-profits policies, which are typically based on a mix of shares, fixed interest and property.

- **Unit-linked annuities**: your annuity tracks a predetermined unit trust portfolio, which means it could go down (you don't own units – they are simply a means of measurement).

- **Self-invested annuities**: generally rated the riskiest of all – your annuity depends on your (or your adviser's) investment judgment.

Unless you are seriously rich, you should not consider making your annuity depend on unit trusts or investment choice. But if you placed a large part of your pension fund in a classic, fixed-interest annuity, then some money could go into one or other of these variants.

BUYING AN ANNUITY

Details on choosing and buying an annuity would probably fill another book, but one point stands out: this is one case where it will probably make sense to take professional advice. The Internet will provide a good deal of information, but the insurance companies which sell annuities will not as a rule charge you less if you go direct: they build commission into the price.

A further thought: this is a complex area, and if problems arise later, after you employed an adviser, you will have someone to contact – even to sue.

Now, many of the discount brokers (those who sell you unit trusts and ISAs on better terms) will help. If your affairs or your objectives are at all complicated, then you will have to go to one of the specialist firms. As always, shop around and compare quotes: you may find yourself dealing with significant differences.

Glossary

A guide to the jargon which you will read in the newspapers, hear from an investment adviser and find in books like this.

Asset allocation how you spread your money across different investments, including equities, bonds and cash.

Asset value the market value of securities at a particular date, generally expressed per share or unit or the value of a share in terms of net fixed assets and stock.

Bare trust a trust to hold assets for children until they reach 18, when they automatically assume ownership.

Bear market where there are consistent falls in share prices, and the general expectation that there are further falls to come.

Bid-offer spread in a unit trust, the difference between the buying and selling price – OEICs have just a single price.

Bond a fixed interest security, generally with a predetermined repayment date, issued by governments and companies.

Bull market opposite of a bear market, where share prices are rising and expected to go on rising.

Closed-end fund a fund which has a fixed number of shares, such as an investment trust.

Coupon the rate of interest, expressed as a percentage, which is payable on a bond or government security.

Dead cat bounce a limited recovery in share prices during a bear market – as opposed to a return to a bull market.

Dividend yield the income paid on an investment, generally an ordinary share, expressed as a percentage of its capital value.

Equities ordinary shares – technically, where there is no limit to their share of profits or capital.

Gearing debts of a company expressed as a percentage of its total net assets – gearing varies in different businesses, property companies being normally highly geared; (also known by its US equivalent, 'leverage').

Gilts or gilt-edged securities issued by the British government.

Hedge fund a fund that may employ a range of techniques to enhance return, e.g. both buying and shorting shares.

HMRC Her Majesty's Revenue and Customs since the two organisations merged: HMRC is not yet well known – Inland Revenue has been used throughout this book.

ICVC investment company with variable capital, similar to an OEIC, with a single price.

Independent financial adviser a qualified and regulated professional, who is not tied to any financial group and will be paid by fees and/or commission;

Investment trusts also known as 'closed end' funds that buy other companies' shares – by contrast with unit trusts they have a fixed number of shares and can borrow.

Market capitalisation the market value of a company's capital, often applied to the ordinary capital, where it equals share price times number of shares in issue.

NASDAQ the US stock market for tech stocks, literally National Association of Securities Dealers Automated Quotation System.

OEIC a unit trust, with up-dated procedures, such as a single price and the absence of a trustee (Open-Ended Investment Company: see following).

Open-ended fund or investment company a fund which varies in size depending on whether money is being added or withdrawn, such as a unit trust.

PET potentially exempt transfer – gifts made during your lifetime which will be free of inheritance tax so long as you live for at least seven years, with a reduced rate payable if you live for at least three years.

Price-earnings ratio (P/E) an important tool of investment analysis, which relates the ordinary share price to the earnings expressed as pence per share – showing the number of years' profits an investor is buying. A high P/E in principle suggests that the shares are expensive, and a low P/E that they are good value.

Rate the key lending/borrowing rate – base rate in the UK, set by the Bank of England, and the Federal funds rate in the US decided by the Federal Reserve.

Redemption yield the annualised return on a fixed-interest bond, which allows for any capital gain or loss which will be realised when the bond matures.

Running yield income, generally interest on a bond, expressed as a percentage of the current price, i.e. the income you will in fact receive before any capital profit/loss.

Split-capital trust a fund with a fixed life and different classes of shares, generally including income shares and capital shares.

Stagflation a term used by economic commentators to describe a situation of inflation occurring at a time of low growth.

Take-over bid where a company offers shares or cash to buy control of another. Takeovers are subject to elaborate City rules, e.g. that the offer must be open for at least 21 days. In general, avoid remaining a minority shareholder in a company where there has been a change of control.

Top-down a method employed by fund managers, starting with an analysis of overall political and economic prospects as a way to value particular companies' shares.

Tracker fund a unit trust (sometimes an investment trust) which invests to perform in line with a particular stock market index, also known as index funds – normally low-cost.

Yield gap a widely used market analysis, which represents the difference between the average yield on shares and the average yield on bonds or government securities. A narrow yield gap is considered favourable for equities, as you are being asked to pay relatively little for equities' growth prospects. A wide yield gap can point to lower share prices, as you are being asked to pay a relatively large premium for equities' potential while higher bond yields make them more attractive to investors.

Zero coupon applied to preference shares in the UK and company/government bonds in the US. No interest is paid, but the security is redeemed, at a fixed price, at a fixed time.

Index

How To Books are available through all good bookshops, or you can order direct from us through Grantham Book Services.

Tel: +44 (0) 1476 541080
Fax: +44 (0) 1476 541061
Email: *orders@gbs.tbs-ltd.co.uk*

Or via our website

www.howtobooks.co.uk

To order via any of these methods please quote the title(s) of the book(s) and your credit card number together with its expiry date.

For further information about our books and catalogue, please contact:

How To Books
Spring Hill House
Spring Hill Road
Begbroke, Oxford OX5 1RX

Visit our website at

www.howtobooks.co.uk

Or you can contact us by email at *info@howtobooks.co.uk*